Swindler

A.E. Dawson and *The Canadian Problem*

Leslie Y. Dawson

One Printers Way
Altona, MB R0G 0B0
Canada

www.friesenpress.com

Copyright © 2022 by Leslie Y. Dawson
First Edition — 2022

This book includes the original writing of A. Ernest Dawson, the subject of the story.

Author photo courtesy of Thomas Dawson.

Cover photo courtesy of Kingston Penitentiary Museum, Kingston, Ontario.

All rights reserved.

No part of this publication may be reproduced in any form, or by any means, electronic or mechanical, including photocopying, recording, or any information browsing, storage, or retrieval system, without permission in writing from FriesenPress.

ISBN
978-1-03-911839-3 (Hardcover)
978-1-03-911838-6 (Paperback)
978-1-03-911840-9 (eBook)

1. BIOGRAPHY & AUTOBIOGRAPHY, CRIMINALS & OUTLAWS
2. CANADIAN HISTORY

Distributed to the trade by The Ingram Book Company

Table of Contents

Foreword	v
Chapter 1: Memories and Second-Hand Accounts	1
Chapter 2: A Childhood of Neglect and Abuse	7
Chapter 3: Derbyshire: Learning to be a Farmer	15
Chapter 4: Passage to Canada	29
Chapter 5: Young, Ambitious, and In Love	37
The Great Wheelbarrow Race	49
Chapter 6: Married Life and Success in Business	55
Lizzie, the First Car	66
Chapter 7: The 1920s and The Toronto Casualty Years	71
Chapter 8: Literary Ambitions	85
A Happy Day in Rosedale	91
Chapter 9: The Cataclysm—1929	95
The Dawson Legacy in Canadian Casualty Insurance	100
Chapter 10: The Securities Game in the 1930s	105
Dawson Mining Stock Activities During the 1930s	111
Chapter 11: The Ontario Operations	119
Chapter 12: *The Canadian Problem*	*133*

Chapter 13: Partner in Crime: John Woolcott Forbes	145
Warrant Charges in OSC Extradition Request	150
Chapter 14: The New York Operations	155
The U.S. Indictments	162
Chapter 15: The Mexican Adventure: Part 1	165
Chapter 16: Kidnapped to Texas: Mexican Adventure Part 2	181
Chapter 17: Trials and Punishment	193
Chapter 18: The Orkis Novel—Ernest Looks Back	203
Epilogue	213
Glossary	221

Foreword

Dry, curled oak leaves lay carelessly on one corner of the granite gravestone. My grandfather's name, *A. Ernest Dawson*, was carved into the stone. Here lay the man I had been researching and writing about for two years. This was what was left of him—bones buried in a modest grave in a Kingston, Ontario, cemetery.

Unexpectedly, I dropped to my knees and wept.

"Oh, Grandad!" I whispered.

What a life he had lived! He landed in Canada penniless and rose to the wealthy heights of Toronto society and the Canadian insurance industry. Then he lost it all. After that he became a mining stockbroker, a stock fraudster, and a prisoner in both Canada and the United States. In the end, a lonely old man, he wrote a love story, apparently at peace.

I wept because his story swept across victory and defeat, honour and shame, love and rejection. I wondered if he could see me kneeling at his grave. Kneeling there, I wished for his permission to tell his story.

As the tears ran down my cold cheeks on that sunny, winter afternoon, I felt he wanted me to tell his whole story, not just the good parts. And he whispered to me, as the cold breeze stirred the brittle, brown leaves on the granite stone, that people should know how a smart, ethical man could come to be a Canadian stock market crook. People *should* know, he told me that day, how pride, desperation and temptation could turn a respected captain of industry into a tawdry fraudster, albeit a big one. And how, in the end, he tried to tell his story through writing. He could bring himself to tell only the good parts, the funny bits, but my job was to tell the rest. I am a journalist, and he would respect that.

I knew he wanted me to tell his love story, how he wooed and won Lynda Knight to be his wife of more than sixty years. How she raised his six children largely in his absence. She was his wife, through his humble beginnings, the heights of his glory days, and his imprisonment, finally lying in this same graveyard in separate, lonely graves.

I sensed he wanted me to clear the air at last, to tell what was for decades a deep, shameful family secret. How he defrauded widows, retired farmers, and New York socialites of half a million dollars. How, during World War II, he wasn't "away at the army"—as the family told their friends and neighbours—but languishing in the notorious Kingston Penitentiary. And how his disgrace ended many of his family's dreams and aspirations.

So here I am, telling you, the reader, the story of Alfred Ernest Dawson, a gentleman, a visionary businessman, and an audacious Canadian crook. It is his story, but mine too. The story of my discoveries, disillusionment, and finally, forgiveness. With the help of his own writings, my grandfather and I tell this story together.

LYD

CHAPTER 1:
Memories and Second-Hand Accounts

My siblings, my cousins, and I are the only living people who can now remember meeting Grandad, Mr. Alfred Ernest Dawson. These contacts, brief and long ago, and the second-hand accounts of our parents, comprise all the direct experience we have left of him. The sparse memories and accounts have become "the stuff of legends," according to cousin Ken Howard.

Grandad, for better and for worse, was a remarkable man.

My sister Wendy and brother Timothy both heard that Grandad was, at various times, a millionaire. Now, that's not unusual—rich ancestors figure in many Canadian ancestral stories. But Grandad was the real thing, apparently. His family lived in a huge home in the posh neighbourhood of Rosedale, Toronto. They lived next door to the millionaire who built Casa Loma, the only real castle built in North America. Wendy was proud of her millionaire grandfather. Timothy repeated the legend. "I heard that Grandad made a fortune, lost it, and then made another one," he says. "And I heard that he took a fall for a crooked partner, and ended up in jail."

Jail was a remote, abstract idea for our respectable, white, middle-class family. We didn't know any of the details, except that my father, Don Dawson, said vaguely that it had something to do with mining stocks. Grandad was a stockbroker. But all of us cousins believed that Grandad could not, surely,

1

have done anything *really* wrong. In our minds he was a slightly romantic figure, perhaps a Robin Hood sort of guy.

In fact, cousin Ken recalls his mother Darrell telling him that Grandad was "a great man." She adored her father. But, Ken says, she was both proud and ashamed of him. His fall from grace, after all, had cost her an education in a fine girls' private school, a university education, and a position in high society. Whenever Darrell talked of her father, Ken says, it was with a kind of twisted pride. "Oh, Dad was an outlaw!"

Ken's sister, cousin Phyllis Horne, also recalls growing up perceiving her Grandad through Darrell's eyes. "He was an exciting, wonderful guy," Phyllis remembers her mother telling her. "The most amazing person on earth. Brilliant, loving, caring, exciting, adventurous, musical, literary and intellectual, according to Mum."

Grandad's trouble with the law was never really discussed in the family. Phyllis says, "If he was up to any kind of nefarious business, he could apparently be forgiven. It was somehow excusable... there was no judgment against him—and we weren't all that interested in finding out what he did wrong. I thought it was tax evasion. That he was not hurting anybody. When I found out [what he did] I was quite upset. It was the first time I'd ever heard anything negative about him. Mom was very vague about what he'd done. Maybe she didn't know."

Grandad's hero status persisted despite his behaviour as a gambler and a risk taker. Ken recalls, "We knew he was a gambler. He won a vacation property at the bridge table. And he lost it at another game." Ken adds, "He was not a good husband. He was gone most of the time. But when he came home, he was so exciting for Gram..."

Cousin Peter Howard agrees. He remembers life in the hamlet of Glen Williams, long after the troubles with the law. He says that when Grandad came home from Toronto—on the weekends—Gram could be found happily humming in the kitchen, ready to sit down and play gin rummy for matchsticks in the evening. Peter says that Grandad's presence "lit up her life," even though she had been forced to raise her six children largely alone, including a decade in the shadow of scandal.

My personal memories of Grandad are renewed every Sunday when I serve family dinner on Gram's Blue Willow China set, now maybe a hundred years old. I think the set was a wedding gift, after their years-long courtship through the mail. Grandad saved all their letters, sent nearly every day while he was on the road as an insurance salesman. Their marriage lasted more than sixty years, with Gram raising their six children alone, except during the twenties in Rosedale.

During my childhood, Grandad, then quite elderly, made occasional forays into the West, where my father Don and my Aunt Darrell raised their families. I remember his tall frame and white hair, and he was always dressed impeccably in a dark blue wool suit. As a little girl, I remember the pungent smell of pipe tobacco around him. Once, when I was maybe ten years old, he sat me on his knee and read poetry to me. He pulled down a volume from Dad's bookshelf and read poems of nineteenth-century American poet John Greenleaf Whittier. Whittier was known for his fervent, anti-slavery writings.

Grandad read the poems in his deep, resonant voice. I did not understand the poetry but was captivated by its sound. It was the first time I realized that the English language could be so beautiful. That evening, while I was sitting on his knee, Grandad bequeathed to me the gift of language, of song, of rhythm. It was a gift that has lasted me a lifetime.

Ken recalls that his mother taught him, from Grandad, the importance of being able to recite poetry from memory.

Indeed, Grandad was known by all his grandchildren as a stickler for proper English usage. The Queen's English. On that same visit, Grandad weighed in on my parents' current language campaign. They were fighting our use of the word "yeah" when we should have said "yes."

Grandad leaned his tall frame over and told me, again in his deep voice, "Leslie, the most beautiful thing a woman can say to a man is 'Yes!'"

I never forgot that lesson, and only in later years considered its many possible meanings. But I can still hear him saying it, as if it were yesterday.

Grandad insisted on good behaviour. My cousin Peter spent several weeks every summer at Glen Williams. He said that Grandad never raised his hand against a child, but that "I learned to be on my best behaviour when Grandad was around, and to use correct English."

Both Ken and my father remember the peculiar way Grandad taught swimming. Ken says, "He tied a rope around my waist and threw me into the Credit River," which ran behind the house in Glen Williams. The experience was traumatic, Ken says. Dad got the same lesson at the lake as a boy. They both learned—fast—how to swim.

All of us Western cousins remember Grandad's famous flash visits from Toronto. He would fly in from Toronto and show up at Darrell's or Don's houses without warning, knocking at the door. He would come in, stay for a few minutes, then leave. We had the impression that he was making a brief inspection of his two children's families… we were alive, well, and leading good, middle-class lives. The visits left us with the impression of an important, mysterious man whom we never got a chance to know. And now, looking back, a man who had lost the ability for close, personal relationships, even with his children.

Ken recalls one such whirlwind visit. "On Christmas Day, a taxi pulled up midday, and he arrived. He stayed five minutes and was gone again."

Wendy Dawson, my younger sister, remembers, "He rang the doorbell and informed me that he was my grandfather. I didn't recognize him, of course. Excited, I invited him in. I told him that Mom and Dad were out shopping but they would be back soon. Could I get him a cup of coffee? He said, 'No that's okay.' He came in for ten minutes, looked around, and went back out to the taxi waiting in the driveway. He didn't even wait for Mom and Dad to come home."

Timothy remembers another such visit. "Mom gave him a cup of coffee. He never sat down. I remember that he was looking out the front window. He looked at his watch and said, 'Okay, it's time to go.' And left."

Jim saw the same visit, but a child's observation. "He sat on a high stool and talked with Dad. I wanted to hear what he had to say. But even at that young age, I thought it [the visit] was very odd."

My father, Don, clearly had mixed feelings about his father. He told us that on one hand, Grandad was that necessary cog in the capitalist system—a good salesman. "The world needs salesmen," he told us. He told Jim that Grandad was witty and often spoke "with shock value. He saw things with a twist. He had a positive point of view, and he could get things done."

My dad took possession of Grandad's trunk of papers after his death. This was a large, Chinese, wooden trunk, made of oak with decorative woodwork on its ends. The trunk absorbed many hours of my father's time. He spent the time organizing the thousands of pages of Grandad's writings and clippings.

These included his personal correspondence with Gram (including her letters to him), his magazine articles, his book reviews, his diaries, and his fiction manuscripts. There were also articles written about him during his heyday in the insurance industry.

When I inherited the wooden trunk's contents at Dad's death, I was overwhelmed by the work Dad had done. He had grouped the thousands of papers into sixty categories and made notations on each, summarizing the contents. I looked over the papers after Dad died and realized that for all these thousands of pages, there were no clues as to Grandad's criminal past. The trunk contained only positive materials, although there were a couple of essays about his imprisonment in Mexico and his three hundred pages of prison writings.

But nothing about why he was in prison.

It so happens that I am a journalist, with a lifetime of writing for small newspapers, magazines, and science/medical materials. One thing I know how to do is research. Thus, I set out to fill in the blanks left by Grandad's trunk—the things my father could not bear to tell us about his father.

This book is the result of that work, reading the trunk's materials, and searching in Canadian and U.S. newspapers and books to discover the missing pieces.

What on earth had Grandad done to deserve four years in the notorious Kingston Penitentiary?

And how had such an upright, respectable man become a criminal?

I had to find out.

LYD

CHAPTER 2:
A Childhood of Neglect and Abuse

A.E. Dawson saved everything in his wooden trunk. His earliest document is a negative photostat of his birth certificate. He was born October 2, 1887, in the outskirts of London, the District of Pancras, on 66 Hampstead Road. Today, Hampstead Road is near the major attractions of London, including the British Library.

Ernest arrived, the second of four children, during the foment of the Second Industrial Revolution. It was a decade of great change and technological innovation: a time when trains suddenly linked the great cities of the world, when the first submarines were developed, when the first automobile appeared, and when AC power was first harnessed for use in streetlights and inside buildings. It was also the decade when Europe divided up Africa—and much of the rest of the world—into manageable, colonial islands, and when four political assassinations rocked European and American calm. And, incidentally, during the year of Ernest's birth, John Stith Pemberton invented Coca-Cola, complete with stimulating coca leaves and kola nuts, as a home remedy.

As a child of the 1880s, it is not surprising that Ernest started life as a restless, risk-taking spirit. The world burst with excitement, and London stood at the centre of it all.

Ernest's father, Frederick Henry Dawson, supported his family as a commercial traveller, according to Ernest's birth certificate. He was a travelling salesman, neither a very practical man nor a particularly good breadwinner. This and other details of Ernest's early life come from a biography of Ernest's sister Daisy, *Daisy: The Story of an English War Bride 1886-1970*, by her daughter Pamela Rogers.

Henry was not well educated, but he was an avid reader and valued books highly. This love of literature was, perhaps, the most significant legacy he passed on to his son. Decades later, Ernest wrote to his father that, for his birthday, he would just like some of his father's books.

Henry and his wife Ellen Dawson (*née* Mary Ellen Aulick) bore four children, Ernest being born after his sister Daisy Ellen. Throughout his life, Ernest went by his second name, not his first, Alfred. After Ernest, Winifred May and Violet Madge, his younger siblings, were born.

Henry and Ellen shared two passions—amateur theatre and the Swedenborgian New Church. They were so involved in these activities that Daisy reported hardly knowing her mother, who died of tuberculosis when Ernest was eight. Daisy said that the children were largely ignored by their mother because she was so involved in theatre and the church.

Nevertheless, Ernest retained loving memories of Ellen, his biological mother. Daisy said he displayed "a large photograph of her in his room in Toronto and I'm sure he had kept it near him always." The photo survived in his trunk many years later. Much later in life, he cared for his feckless father with patience and kindness.

The family church was the New Church, founded a century before by the Scandinavian theologian Emanuel Swedenborg. The church somehow combined Swedenborg's unique mystical visions of heaven and hell with a strict, fundamentalist moral code. Swedenborg was a scientist who in the last fifteen years of his life claimed to have constant intercourse with the spirit world. His book, *Heaven and Its Wonders and Hell*, is a detailed description of these "firsthand" revelations.

Daisy remembered having to go to church three times each Sunday and described Henry and Ellen's devotion as "excessive and neurotic." She describes her own—and Ernest's—childhood as having a background of high moral purpose in the context of a disintegrating family life.

Daisy recalled few joys in her early life. Ernest seems to have agreed. Later in life, in his notes from jail, he said he could remember only *one* incident of kindness in his entire childhood! It was his earliest memory, he said, and involved being run over on the street in London, somewhere near his home on Hampstead Road. He must have darted across the street and was knocked down by a milk cart horse and run over by a cartwheel. He remembered being carried upstairs to the bedroom of a nearby house and being wrapped about by what seemed to him miles and miles of flannel. He remembered several people as being very kind.

Things only got worse. Not long after his mother Ellen's death, Henry remarried a widow with three children. Ernest described her later as "that dreadful woman, the step[mother]." Daisy recalled this second wife as being the "wicked stepmother" who was never accepted by the four original Dawson siblings. Even years later, Ernest disliked this woman when she came to Canada. Neither Ernest nor Daisy ever names the stepmother.

I can only imagine that Ernest's childhood as an environment of excessive discipline, perhaps bordering on abuse. The stepmother probably ignored the four Dawsons in favour of her own children. At any rate, Daisy says that Ernest started running away from home at some time in his childhood. She said he searched for her when she was sent away to boarding school. Daisy's biographer notes, "These days we recognize that running away from home is a sign of depression in a child, but in those days it was regarded as sheer perversity and punished accordingly."

From Daisy's recollection of the Dawson children's upbringing, one might not be surprised at some of Ernest's later issues as an adult. He too was an absentee father, a travelling insurance salesman, later living in Toronto during the week, or travelling on business. He came home on weekends. He certainly had trouble conducting close relationships with his children and grandchildren.

A friend of mine, clinical psychologist Sarah Berger, suggests that his childhood might also have set the stage for a man who was constantly trying to prove himself worthy of love and attention... a man who had something to prove.

Some researchers believe that environmental factors, or "root causes," result in criminal behaviour. Stanton E. Samenow, in *Inside the Criminal*

Mind, says, "Virtually everything imaginable has been identified as a cause of criminal behaviour, including poverty, bad parenting, peer pressure, violence in the media, and various types of mental illness... None of the widely accepted causes of crime withstood scrutiny."

In the case of Ernest Dawson, poverty might have been a factor—his family was certainly not wealthy, perhaps ranking on the lower levels of the middle class. Like many in that era, Ernest went to work early in his teens—actually at the age of twelve. A case could also be made for poor parenting in Ernest's case. His parents seemed to combine religion-based authoritarianism along with outright neglect. However, cruel parenting and neglect did not stop him from high achievement later on.

Whatever the flaws in his upbringing, Ernest certainly learned to read and to think. At the age of twelve he took work as a printer's devil—a general assistant in a print shop. In this shop, he met writers of the time, including G.K. Chesterton. In a letter to a friend, much later in life, he recalled Chesterton as a flamboyant, colourful character.

In a 1901 job, when he was fourteen, Ernest worked at a pharmaceutical manufacturer (making knife polish, vermin killer, silver polish, and metal paste, among other things). His employer gave him a good, if understated, reference. "Ernest Dawson has been in our employ six months. He is a sharp, intelligent boy and we have found him honest and fairly industrious," wrote managing director H.E. Welch.

Soon after Henry's remarriage to the wicked stepmother, Ernest's sister Daisy reports that the Dawson children all resolved to escape to Canada. Daisy took up training as a nurse. Ernest, on the other hand, seems to have noticed that England was plastered with posters urging Britons to emigrate to the rich agricultural lands of Canada. Huge posters showed fields of golden grain and rich farmland.

Ernest wrote an unpublished novel late in life, *In the Shadow of Orkis*. Like the character George in his novel, Ernest moved to the rural countryside of Derbyshire. In the novel, George deliberately set out to learn how to be a farmer. Both Ernest's memoirs and fiction tell of how he, like George, was a city boy from London who became a skilled cattle drover and a valued, hardworking farmhand. If Canada needed farmers, Ernest could be a farmer!

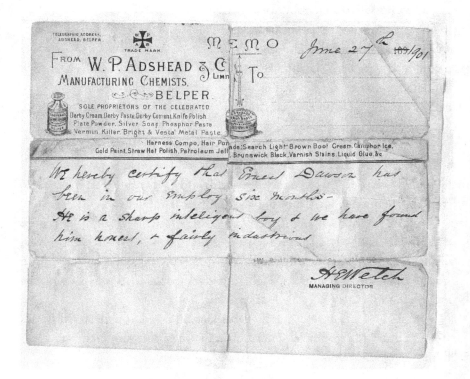

A job reference from one of A.E. Dawson's first employers

Who at this time was Ernest Dawson, the protagonist of our story? He starts out, in his late teens, as an innocent, open, and kind young man. This we can tell from his account of working as a farm labourer, probably in his mid-to-late teens. His lengthy memoir of this period shows that he worked hard and played equally hard, an energetic youth. This account comes from a handwritten notebook in the wooden trunk, labelled Number 9 by my father, Don. According to occasional dates in the manuscript, he probably wrote the memoir in 1911, perhaps ten years after the actual events took place. At the time of writing, Ernest was in the insurance business. For our purposes in the coming chapter, we have excerpted the manuscript, re-ordered passages somewhat, and added punctuation or spelling to clarify the writing. We have preserved Ernest's rather wordy, Victorian style of writing.

Ernest possessed a city boy's observations and appreciation of bucolic life. In the memoir, he describes the tough daily work in a rugged landscape, and his first pleasant encounters with women— "the lassies." This account provides us with the "baseline Ernest," from which he grows in experience and changes in morality over the coming years. It is worth reading his story here, to see how far he evolved from this innocence to the worldly man of finance and fraud in decades to come.

At this time, Ernest lived in and near the town of Derby, in Derbyshire, a county in the East Midlands region of England. The area was remote and hilly, and was devoted to agriculture and mining at the time. Today, the county contains a large part of the Peak District National Park.

Ernest describes walking through the Derbyshire County on the way to church. He recalls the road through the landscape as "a most delightful part of the country, past romantic old farms, through a quaint village… and in summer past rows of heavily laden fruit trees, so numerous as to be commonplace to the people in the locality."

Ernest's next memory of the time was a chance encounter in town (probably Derby) with a young lady in trouble. He was nearly crippled with bashfulness in contacting her.

> I was looking into a shop window about 10 o'clock one Saturday evening and heard a sob from someone at my side. I found a girl of about 15 years of age silently crying and my bashfulness for some time threatened to overcome my correct desire to learn if I could help her. I had started to go away twice and returned then, trembling like a leaf. I addressed her in a broken fashion and after a long time I extracted the information from her that she was a country girl living some few miles out of town. She had driven in with someone who was not returning but a storm had come on preventing her from walking back, as she had intended, and… it was a black night and last train was about to go and she lacked a half penny for her railway fare. And in her ignorance of town life and her ignorance of traveling also, she was in a terrible plight. Too much afraid of the dark and stormy night to attempt to walk… and having no friends in town, she seemed to herself a hopeless case. While she was wiping her eyes, and could not see

me I slipped my hand into my pocket and not daring to insult her by giving her a bit more than she needed, I got a half penny out and thrust it into her hand and scampered off as fast as my legs would carry me, as though I had committed some heinous crime, but rejoicing that I had been able to relieve the girl from her misfortune. Weeks after, whenever I thought of her, a lump would rise in my throat and I would feel strangely stirred. I have never to my knowledge seen her since.

From this account, in his teens, the painfully shy Ernest could certainly feel empathy. Lack of empathy is a key factor in the development of the criminal personality, according to many criminal psychologists. Samenow says, "Criminals... do not seem to resonate to other human beings, in that they show no empathy and are indifferent to the suffering that they cause." In Ernest's case, if he ever lacked empathy, the flaw developed later in his life, in the business world. At this time, Ernest was an innocent who could certainly feel another's pain and wanted to help.

CHAPTER 3:
Derbyshire: Learning to be a Farmer

Once in Derbyshire, Ernest set to work learning how to be a farmer. I think he saw this as the next step needed to get out of England. I don't think he ever lost sight of this goal during his teen years while he herded cattle, shovelled manure, tended crops and hung out with the "lads and lassies" after work. He was a hard worker, and a good learner.

He first took employment as a drover with a gentleman named John Brassington. A drover was, essentially, a cowboy on foot, moving herds of cattle from farm to farm, and back and forth to market. He describes the work in memoirs, written some years later.

> I gained a great deal of experience here. J. Brassington was a character well known in the town and did as I have said a very varied business. Anyone with a dying animal for sale was sure of finding a market for it at J. Brassington's, where it would quickly be converted into beef for the troops... or some other unsuspecting body of humans who were fed under government contract...
>
> Cattle would usually arrive at night under cover of darkness and often at midnight would I have to turn out and help convert these wretched specimens of "prime" beef. Mr. Brassington was a man of hasty temperament and often ordered certain things done, which afterwards he might have wished undone.

Ernest boasted that in all the herds he drove along dark, foggy, hedged-in roads, he never lost an animal. He said this feat was "well nigh impossible," but he managed it somehow. He often drove twenty to a hundred animals, usually without the help of a dog. Dark-coloured animals and calves were easy to miss, slipping into ditches and along side roads, but he never lost one. He said, indeed, "I should feel proud" of this record.

The drover experience gave Ernest confidence to look for work in rural areas.

His next job, as a general farmhand, was with Mr. Herbert Woodurise, an area businessman and sometime farmer. In his memoirs, Ernest paints a fond and detailed picture of his new life in the countryside.

> Mr. W. combined the carpenter's and wheelwright's business with dairying and agriculture and desiring to have more time for the former businesses, he had decided to get someone to look after his farm. Hence my advent. A man of some thirty-two or three, wife and no children, in very moderate circumstances, hasty-tempered and rather inconsistent in manner, yet withal possessed of a generous soul, many more ideas than he carried out, proud of his wife, his house and his belongings—such was Mr. W., who was to take care of my physical needs and add somewhat to my pocket in return for my assistance on the farm, having already had some experience among cattle.

Ernest proved a competent hire for Mr. Woodurise. He claimed in his memoir that his cattle experience proved superior to Mr. W's. "In fact, it was not long ere I found that I knew considerably more about the best interest of dairying etc. than he did. In the matter of crops, however, he had a superior knowledge to mine, as a sort of complement, I suppose." Ernest got down to work, feeding the cows, fencing, and tending the sheep.

> The milk had to be taken to the cheese factory at Hope Dale, which factory was built right in the stream at the base of the dale, part of the stream flowing continually through the factory. The water was always ice cold, and coming as it did from springs in the peaks of Derbyshire, it made an ideal cooler for the factory. Morning and night this factory was the meeting place of numerous farm hands

and milkmaids, amounts of milk varying from the product of one cow to thirty being taken in from individual customs.

Ernest soon exhausted the possibilities for growth with Mr. Woodurise. He kept his ears open for other opportunities and went for them. After picking a quarrel with Mr. Woodurise, he moved to the farm of Mr. Ralph Adams of Narrowdale, about four miles away, near the border of Staffordshire.

This move illustrates Ernest's lifelong pattern of ever seeking his fortune at ever higher levels and responsibilities. From then on, for most of his life, Ernest was a man on the move, seeking more challenges, and always more money.

> [Someone] told me that Mr. Adams needed help and had advised me to go and offer myself. Mr. Adams was minding the large farmland when I presented myself... I wanted seven shillings for week and he offered four... I closed with him for six shillings per week and I believe commenced work that day...

> Mr. Adams, or "Rafe" Adams (Ralph is invariably pronounced Rafe in that district) was a man of fifty or thereabout, a kindly disposition and well-meaning man. Two of his sons, grown up men, worked with him on the farm. A daughter of about twenty, a beautiful healthy girl, helped her mother in housekeeping, and a younger girl of about fifteen, going to school, completed the household except for some various servants and a farm hand named Sam Salt. Salt and I quickly became good friends, working together when we had to, loafing together whenever we could, getting into whatever mischief together was possible—or advisable—and spending our spare time and Sundays together at neighboring villages among lads and lassies of his acquaintance whom he, being bred and born in the neighborhood, numbered quite a few.

The work was hard and continuous. Ernest describes it in detail.

> There were some buildings for the cattle to enter at will during three seasons out of four, and which in winter sheltered the young cattle and milking cows and up which we had to climb often

through several feet of snow to feed, milk and tend the cattle generally. This occasioned many hardships during cold evenings in the dark (for it grew dark there about four o'clock in winter) such as wading through the snow, falling over large boulders when one got off the cow path, carrying the milk or drawing it on wheels down to the dairy at the house. This milk was taken every evening during winter and every morning and evening during the summer, but each usually awaited the others' return in order that we might take a jaunt somewhere together for the night.

It was certainly not all work and no play for Ernest. He enjoyed the company of his friends and co-workers and played as hard as he worked. I think he was a typical teen of the times. He stayed up all night playing games and storytelling with friends, and ate as much hearty country food as he could. I know from family anecdotes that he loved playing cards all his life… this period was the first, perhaps, where he indulged in such games regularly. In later years, he became a frequent and devoted bridge player, often for high stakes. And he became a gambler in many other ways, willing to take increasingly high risks with investments and his businesses.

Ernest was clearly a sociable young man, another pattern that served him well in later life. He makes no mention of alcohol in his goings about, sticking to more innocent habits. My father remembered him as a teetotaller for most of his life.

> Winter was upon us when I went there and in our ramblings together over the hills to some laborer's cottage or other, where Salt's friends would be congregated. We were very glad of some hot tea or cocoa and cakes. We usually stayed playing draughts or cards or telling yarns till five o'clock in the morning when we would strike off for Narrowdale farm and commence work, rarely interfered with by the house folk as to where we spent the night, or because we never got any sleep. This continued all the time I was there and I seldom knew what it was to have a sleep except under a hedge in summer or in a barn in winter when we were supposed to be working and when Mr. A and his sons were away.

At our meals, pudding, being cheaper than meat, always preceded the meal and many times we demolished a suet pudding weighing six to ten pounds with treacle on it before the meal appeared, when we would be pretty much too well satisfied to eat any. We sat at a table by ourselves with our backs to the family table and would often make signs or under-breath remarks concerning the food, which after all was good and plentiful.

Ernest experienced the full range of rural life, from small game hunting to wrangling cattle and tending cabbage fields. As the reader of his memoir of this period, I was fascinated by his descriptions of activities on the farm. These anecdotes seem so distant from the genteel, cultured man that I knew in later years, always in suit and tie.

Frequently we took Sundays off, Sam staying to do necessary work when I was away and I staying while he went away, and after the morning's work was over Herbert (the eldest son) and I would go for a walk over the hills, taking with us some ferret and a gun and shoot some rabbits, or instead of shooting them, net them in bags by placing the nets over several rabbit holes and putting the ferret muzzled down one of the uncovered holes. Once I went to grab a big buck rabbit when he appeared to be getting away with the net and instead he grabbed me, sinking his front teeth right through the flesh portion of my forefinger and I stood there, half scared out of my wits, shaking this big rabbit on one finger and Herbert laughing very heartily meanwhile. I believe I had to eat this one for my vengeance upon it. My finger took quite a long time in healing from the vicious attack.

Spring quickly came around and with it increased activity and commencement of operations for the year's crops. The cattle were turned out night and day. I usually rounded them up from off the hills and brought them into the yard near the house for milking in the summertime, and having to take the milk to Hartingdon I usually brought up the horse with them. One cow gave me some trouble one evening and attempted to go the wrong way. Being a long limbed "rangy" brute she would travel as fast as the horse I rode upon for quite a distance. In this case, she outstripped me into the wrong yard and she led me into a peculiar corner where I could only get at her on foot, which I had to do hurriedly to be in time to prevent her entering the open dairy and pulling the horse short, scarce waiting for him to break from his gallop, I dropped off his bare back on to a square cobble stone and dropped, almost fainting from a sprained ankle in consequence. The cow got into the dairy I believe, but I knew nothing for some time, but the pain from my ankle which was very severely sprained and it began immediately to swell until I had a foot and ankle like a horse with "grassy leg."

The spring passed on. Cow cabbage roots and most seeds were in and doing well, a good spring season. For the benefit of the average Canadian who does not grow cow cabbage, nor is familiar with it at all, I may say to him that these cabbages are usually planted one yard distant from each other and in cross foot fashion, that the harrow may run through them in any direction, but this can only be done during the early part of the season for the cabbage has a rapid growth and quickly takes up the space allotted it in the thirty-six inches and frequently grows to a weight of a hundred pounds although perhaps an average weight would be nearer thirty to forty lbs per cabbage. The cabbage fields on this farm were situated on the high plateau I have before mentioned and a considerable distance from the house. Many times, as Salt and I have grown thirsty at the work—the sun beats down very strongly on those hills—we have drunk our fill of rainwater from some of the broad under-leaves which have carried the water since the previous rainfall. I have many times known these leaves to hold more than a pint of water, so broad and high were they.

For a city boy, Ernest certainly learned the ways of rural life both broadly and intensely. Somehow, he managed to maintain hard farm labour while participating in country fairs and many other recreational activities. I'm not sure how he survived all-night ramblings and hanging out with his friends, but he did, despite being very tired. He was curious and made mental notes of everything he saw.

> We were often frightfully sleepy, to which at this work, the sun seeming to awaken our faculties to the need of sleep, for we kept up the habit of spending seven nights out of the week in revelry as during the winter. My wonder now is that it didn't wreck my constitution irrevocably—certainly it must have done me much harm. Haying time came along and with it still higher increased activity, and of a pleasurable variety. Mr. Adams had several very good meadows and the crops were fair. Harvest weather was good too… everything went well. Fairs were coming on in different parts of the county—horse shows, ploughing matches, sheep dog trials, etc. Cattle selling fairs too, because frequently where markets were distant, a fair would be held in some agreed center, usually being the roadside near some county inn where there would be a sufficient number of cattle to induce dealers to attend in considerable numbers. Much of exciting interest would be for me in these fairs, should I be fortunate enough to be sent, and I usually was because of my knowledge of cattle dealing and the handling of cattle. I would see many of my old acquaintances from the western and southern portion of Derbyshire and the noise, the bustle and activity and change of scene suited my personal feelings very well.
>
> The sheep dog trials, which were being held all over the county, were of interest to me. Herbert Adams had several dogs which were well trained and one of which carried off several fairly good prizes. It is a very interesting hobby, this training of sheep dogs.
>
> Our frequent journeyings out at night are worth a passing mention. During the summer season, there were many small fairs throughout the villages surrounding the locality about which I am writing. These small fairs or "wakes" as they were called would stay for two or three nights at a place, then move on a couple or more miles to the next hamlet and pitch tents, drawing a large crowd of farm lads and lassies who would walk in from distances of one to ten or twelve miles. The chief attraction perhaps was

the foregathering of these crowds and Aunt Sally shows [on-stage, performing side shows], the roundabouts and dancing, [which] gave them a common interest. Salt and I would sally forth as soon as our work was done, meet some more lads at a cross-roads or some other prearranged place of meeting and we would proceed in a body to these wakes where we would single out the lassies we desired to spend the evening with and thus start the fun of evenings. We had the whole of our wages to spend and had no compunction in spending them.

During this period, Ernest seems to have had his first experiences with young women. He clearly enjoyed their company but observed the fate of many of them—and their young men—when the girls got pregnant. He does not mention becoming attached to any particular girl, perhaps keeping his ultimate goal of leaving for Canada in the forefront of his consciousness.

The lassies were well favored girls from neighboring communities, healthy, strong, good-looking girls well able to take care of themselves, yet quietly sweet and companionable. They had learned to be able to stand the round of pleasures all night and going home in the breaking rays of day and doing their day's work without any apparent harm to their constitutions and without any undue sleepiness. Many a girl I have walked home with from these fairs, and any distance from one to six and seven miles, arriving there as the light red and yellow rays of the coming sun were creeping up between the hills and we would bid each other good-bye and make an appointment to meet at the same fair held perhaps that evening at another point maybe several miles distant from the place of previous meeting.

This going to fairs kept up for more than two months and after that the habit had become so strong that we would agree to meet at some laborer's cottage convenient for all (after entailing a long walk for many) and pass the night in song, cards, and various gaming. Having coffee and cakes provided by the hospitable laborer and his wife who were always glad to have us and who always gave us of their best and invited us back when leaving.

There was no chiding because of late hours or dissipation of energies in the dance and song, but a hearty encouragement in the life and song of youth, brief as they knew it to be and harmless as it was in the main.

Life in the days before birth control was chancy. In the memoir, Ernest describes what happened when a girl became pregnant. She and the young man were married immediately, and that was that. I suspect that Ernest refrained from sex to some extent, because he never mentions a particular girl, or the worry of pregnancy in his life. He had a very fundamentalist upbringing, which may have influenced his sexual behaviours, or maybe he was just lucky.

> It cannot be doubted that mistakes were occasionally made and some poor girl suffered for innocent folly, but there was a sort of an unspoken code, crude as it may have been, which in its way met the exigencies of the case and when harm was done it was very seldom indeed that a girl was left to mourn her fate. The unfortunate couple generally were married and speaking from my observation and knowledge of conditions, I can confidently assert that there was a certain method of selection even in this crude form of courting which brought about many happy marriages. They were chiefly ignorant of convictions, their lives were often, pure and innocent and wholesome. Free from guile, knowing little or nothing of the world, their lives were usually spent about their birthplace, knowing nothing of actual want by reason of their habits of life and knowing nothing of the blessings and curses of a greater plenty, which would have taken into their calm and uneventful lives many a note of dissatisfaction and discontent.

While Ernest actively participated in the young people's activities, I sense he held himself apart, as the experienced, better educated and more sophisticated "city boy" from London. Ernest, despite his close companionships in Derbyshire, was an outsider looking in. He describes this in his memoir, aware of his better education and his very different goals in life. He was *with* them, but not *of* them. This alienation, however slight, was perhaps the beginning of another of Ernest's traits. He could use his charm and intelligence to penetrate any group and could act independently of these connections.

> The fact that I had been to "Lunnon", that I had a fair education, and could occasionally use a longer word in conversation, gave me a certain precedence which was enjoyable to me and among the lassies. I had for this reason a fairly easy choice, which although I was not loath to use it, yet because I had made myself one of them, fraternizing with them, entering whole-souled into their enjoyments and not attempting to assume any difference from them, I did not rouse their envy or their ire, but made many friends.

This ability to blend in with any group was no doubt a key factor in Ernest's later success as a salesman. His true feelings about country folk were betrayed, however, in a somewhat condescending, class-based point of view.

> These simple people of the hills spent a life of peaceful ignorance of the rough and tumble turmoil of the world and one of those having been to a city of any importance was held to be a hero and a person of wide experience. Tourists came among them, wealthy people and strangers from all over the country, but they were always held to be entirely distant. If a feeling of envy ever rose in the breasts of these simple good folk it was a feeling of absolutely without hope or conscious desire and as they came, so they went, and the visions were put away to be recalled at the chimney nook of a winter's evening or in the corner of a hay field during a rest hour.

Ernest learned a hard lesson about love from the experience of his friend Salt. I think this lesson may have made him very cautious about his relationships with young women. It may, in fact, have kept him relatively unentangled until he courted Lynda Knight for two years, and married her later in Canada.

> We used to congregate quite frequently at a relative of Salt's… close to the Hulme End Light Railway. This person's house was a little one storey stone hovel with a huge stone fireplace occupying the entire of one end of one room, over which was a mantle

shelf [with] many interesting relics and heirlooms and leading away from the fireplace on each side of the room were wide stone benches for seats and between them in the center of the room was a heavy... table on which we used to have our games or our little meal, and loaf around on Sundays and during nights. The little old couple were kindly and odd creatures. They had with them a sweet little granddaughter of some eighteen years old. Sweet as the very hills she had grown on, with laughing eyes, perfect features and color, and nicely rounded arms and a disposition as beautiful as she was herself. She seemed a delightful vision as she waited upon us at the hovel, serving us with tea of her own brewing and oat cakes of her own baking. Sam Salt and she were fast friends. They were cousins I believe and Sam had no compunction in taking his cousinly privilege and not one of us but envied him his kiss. They grew more and more to each other and his visits there became more and more frequent, and as I was chumming with him and worked at the same place, I of course went with him and watched a tragedy in real life which almost overwhelmed me. The Hulme End Railway had its terminus a few miles from the hovel... A young tourist one day roamed away from this station and lost himself on the hills and came across the little granddaughter, picking cowslips in a meadow... The girl was always a picture of sweetness and cleanliness, dressed in the light print of a dairy maid with arms bare to the elbow and a sun bonnet over her head with strings blowing out over her back.

Evidently the picture fascinated the young man from the city and he in turn fascinated the simple child with his graceful talk and carriage and his description of life in London. It must have charmed her for she disappeared with him and the only news learned of her before I left that region was that she had been seen getting on the train with a stranger at Hulme End.

I left the community shortly after and have since heard no more concerning the event, but poor Sam lost interest in everything. He was no more companionable, no more a lively gay good fellow but stayed around working and working. It was with a very heavy heart I bade him good bye and went back home to Derby.

Ernest's account of his time in Derbyshire ends with another hire.

> J.B. Curling, Grocer, Wine and Spirit Merchant of Derby town wanted a youth to drive his delivery wagon and work in and about the shop and stable. I do not remember the circumstances of my being led thither, but the fact of the employment is prominent in my mind.

For a city boy, he had learned a lot. Did he, though, learn that love could come at a high price? I believe he came out of the experience a cautious young man, holding his heart at bay unless the young woman suited him. The milkmaids of Derbyshire were not his intended or accidental mates. Once again, at the time of writing, he could certainly feel others' pain—he remembered Sam's sadness acutely. At this time, Ernest was a normal, feeling young man, with great sympathies for his compatriots. At the same time, he was separate from them, operating on another level.

It is not clear when from his writings, but during or after learning to be a farmer, Ernest also invested in his formal education. I believe that by educating himself, Ernest was telling us that he had no intention of living out his life as a farmhand. His studies indicate that he had plans for a higher station in life.

He apparently studied at a school under a teacher, Ernest G. Morley of Newton-le-Willows. There are two Newton-le-Willows in England. One is a village in North Yorkshire, another a market town near Liverpool in Merseyside, Lancashire. It is possible that Ernest studied in Merseyside, where he could also learn about immigrant ship passages to Canada.

Mr. Morley wrote a warm note to Ernest just before he set sail to Canada in 1905, wishing him "a safe and pleasant voyage and every success and happiness in your new sphere of life." He added, "I have always found you a very worthy scholar and one which I am really sorry to lose and I feel sure that the knowledge you have acquired while in the school will stand you in good stead." His advice? "Try to act honestly and straight forwardly, trust in God in all your doings and you will eventually triumph."

Although he does not mention it in his memoirs, Ernest saved money from his farm work, just enough to pay for his schooling and his ticket to Canada, with a little spare change. He had prepared himself in many ways to succeed in Canada. He was well-read and educated, intelligent, sociable, and ambitious. He could tell any potential employer that he could handle cattle, dairying, horses, and crops. He was strong physically and a hard worker. That turned out to be enough to start him in a new life as an immigrant.

CHAPTER 4:
Passage to Canada

Having learned about farming from the ground up, Ernest continued his quest to leave England. He clipped a notice from a newspaper in early 1905 (saving it, of course, for the wooden trunk). The article was the announcement of a Salvation Army emigration boat to Canada, set to sail in April 1905. The announcement said:

> Those who are taken out must be of good character, and willing to work and to pay their fares. No alcoholic drinks will be served during the voyage, but there will be smoking room accommodations. The object of the enterprise is to permit people to travel with friends, and it is open to anyone to join the party. It will enable the inexperienced to make friends and cross the ocean under the best social conditions. The fare charged will be £5 10s per adult; children under twelve will be carried at half price … The berths are not all booked yet; about 200 remain. It is astonishing to observe the different classes of people who intend on traveling on this boat—poor labourers, small capitalists, and rich people. One lady is worth £4,000. The reason they join is the sense of security they have in the Salvation Army. They know that the advice they get from them is disinterested and that they will not be robbed by agents on the other side.

All Aboard the SS Vancouver

Ernest must have set aside most of his earnings on the various farms where he worked. It would have taken him two or three years, at six or seven shillings per week, to save up the £5 fare (there are 134 shillings in a pound). Nevertheless, on April 26, 1905, he boarded the Salvation Army immigrant vessel, the SS *Vancouver*, at Liverpool. An undated newspaper article (also in the wooden trunk) noted that

> A ship came over the Atlantic with an all-British passenger list, of whom every man was a prospective Canadian settler, had money for a start, and knew, unlike the average colonist... where he should go and what he should do when he got ashore. It was a larger ship, a larger passenger list, and a larger Canada.

The boat took one thousand immigrants gathered from nearly every part of England, Scotland, and Wales, and was made up of, optimistically, a "more than usually promising class of people."[1]

In the clipping, a photo of a large group of young men appeared. Ernest marked his face on the front row, among the many in the photo. The caption read,

> WAITING TO BE PASSED BY THE DOCTOR Young men from England, Ireland and Scotland, who are bound for the Canadian west. They represent the better class of mechanics and farm labourers and are shown waiting on the S.S. *Vancouver* at Quebec until the doctor has passed them.

Every passenger received a small pamphlet, also in the wooden trunk, announcing that

> In securing this splendid vessel of the Dominion Line for the present voyage across the Atlantic, we desired by bringing together people of kindred spirit to mitigate as far as possible the discomforts which are incidental to such a journey—to promote that feeling of comradeship which is so helpful in life, and to assure the anxious passenger that in choosing his future location he will have the best advice available.

---

[1] *The Weekly Globe and Canada*, "Chapters in Canadian Immigration". Date unknown.

The ship sailed out of Liverpool with a full complement of passengers under Captain J. Evans.

The pamphlet was also full of inspirational, Salvation Army text, including the following advice:

Don't   be easily discouraged.

Be afraid of honest work of any kind.

Allow the devil to fool you.

Be in a hurry to be rich. (Riches have wings)

Forget that when in doubt or difficulty

the Salvationist

will help you as far as he can.

Wait for something to turn up!

A.E. Dawson's ticket to Canada, officiated by Mrs. Booth, wife of the founder of the Salvation Army.

A weekly magazine's photo of Ernest (second from bottom left) and his fellow passengers to Canada.

Landing in Canada: First Job

Despite reading these words many times, Ernest was, indeed, in a hurry to get rich (but in decades to come, discovered that riches, indeed, have wings). When he landed in Quebec City, he also seemed anxious to get as far away from England and go into Canada as far west as he could. He headed west on the train and kept on going until he ran out of money in Lakefield, north of Peterborough in central Ontario. At that point, with twenty-five cents left in his pocket, he got off the train and started looking for work. He was hired as a farm labourer and worked there until the fall.

In 1925, twenty years later, Ernest recounted the story of his early days in Canada to Ashley Austen, in an article for the June 15, 1925, issue of *Maclean's Magazine*[2]. Austen's article is quoted extensively here, since it details Ernest's humble beginnings in Canada when he was just nineteen years old. As he had planned, learning to be a farmer got him started in his new home.

> Now, a quarter of a dollar, whether expressed in terms of cents or pence, doesn't go very far toward keeping life in a hungry, growing boy, who is starting life in a strange land, without home or friends. But it happened that one of Mr. Dawson's strongest characteristics, then, as now, was to go after what he wanted. He wanted a job.
>
> After some hours of dusty hiking along the country roads about the town, stopping at farms and wherever there was likelihood of employment, he met a man on a milk wagon. Dawson stopped him and stated his case. The other gazed quizzically down on him.
>
> "No," he said at length, "I don't need help, but—jump on. Mebbe my brother could use you. I'll drive you over."
>
> They drove for four miles back along the way that Dawson had come. At the farm the brother also favored the applicant with a calculating glance.
>
> "Need a man? Well, mebbe yes, and again mebbe no," he said enlighteningly. "What's your name?"
>
> "Dawson."
>
> "Where are you from?"
>
> "London, England."
>
> "Humph! What have ye been used to doing?"
>
> "I left school before I was twelve and got a job as a printer's devil."
>
> "What good's a printer's devil on my farm?"

---

[2] *MacLean's Magazine*, Austen, Ashley, , "A Twenty-five Cent Start in Life," June 15, 1925, page 18.

"I chucked that to go farming. I worked for a farmer and cattle dealer for three years—until just before I came out here."

"M-hmmm. When did you land?"

"Two days ago."

The farmer smiled. "What made you come out?"

"I wanted to come," he said.

The farmer understood, somehow.

"I'll give you ten dollars a month to stay until after the fall plowing," he said.

And Then, Insurance

Thus, Ernest landed his first job in Canada. The same *Maclean's* article tells his story of how he got into the insurance game. After his contract with the farmer was over in the fall, he took a job with a contractor laying foundation stones for a house, at a dollar and a half a day.

> One afternoon while hard at work he was approached by a neatly dressed man of agreeable manner who introduced himself as Thomas Mark, the Peterboro [*sic*] agent for the Manufacturers Life Insurance Company. A certain policy, which he named and explained, was the one thing certain to put young Dawson on the high road to success. Dawson was interested from the start—not so much in the policy as in the details of it and the other man's method of presenting them. A thought leaped into his head, and as his prehensile brain reached out and grasped the fundamentals of what the insurance man was saying before the other was quite done, he felt a mental stimulation which he had never before experienced. One thing at a time, however—and he was supposed to be working.

"I've got to get this job through," he told the other, "but if you like I'll meet you at six o'clock tonight, and we'll talk it over some more."

Shortly after the other man had gone, Dawson's employer came around to see how the work was progressing and the young man told him of the agent's visit. The contractor snorted.

"Don't you put your good money into no insurance schemes, my boy," he advised. "You steer clear of them fellows or they'll skin you. Put your money into houses! That's what I did and look at me. Build and be rich—that's my motto. You do what I tell you and never mind these fancy schemes."

Dawson grinned to himself. He couldn't build very extensively on what remained from a dollar-fifty a day nor would it buy much insurance. However that didn't prevent him from thinking what he would do if he had the money.

At six o'clock he met the insurance man. As a result of his thought during the afternoon Dawson was able to discuss the proposition with a soundness of opinion and intelligence that caused the other considerable astonishment.

"Good heavens, man!" he said at length, "You're wasting time laying stone. You ought to be out selling insurance!" Probably it did not occur to either of them that young Dawson was laying a foundation in a double sense but the remark crystallized what had been in the boy's mind for most of the afternoon.

"Do you think I have a chance?" he asked.

"Come and see me in the morning and I'll give you a start," the other told him.

This is how Ernest describes his first step into the world of insurance and high finance. He turned out to be an excellent salesman and then an even more successful entrepreneur in insurance and securities.

CHAPTER 5:
Young, Ambitious, and In Love

Ernest was good at selling insurance. So good, in fact, that he was soon one of the top salesmen for his company. He quickly established a professional life for himself in Canada and began to lay the groundwork for his future in Canadian society.

In less than a year after setting foot in Canada, Ernest was, like his father before him, a travelling salesman. However, Ernest was selling something he believed in, and something that the Canadian public was just beginning to understand. Life insurance had become popular as a way for the middle class to save money and to ensure the security of their survivors. It made sense to people at a time when there were no such things as pensions, old age security, RRSPs, or mutual funds. Life insurance was one of the only ways for a farmer—or a store owner—to assure the well-being of his wife and family after he died. It was a way for the middle class to acquire modest wealth.

Ernest travelled the small communities north and west of Toronto, working for a series of large firms, including Manufacturers Life Insurance (now MONY) and Imperial Life Insurance. He had the gift of gab, and he was charming and persistent. He worked hard at it. He was good at selling insurance.

Ernest's first insurance employer was Manufacturers Life Insurance Company, established in 1887 by Sir John A. MacDonald and Ontario's lieutenant governor, Sir Alexander Campbell. The company amalgamated with the Temperance and General Life Assurance Company in 1901, offering preferred rates to abstainers of alcohol. The company survives today as Canada's largest insurance company, Manulife. The company is now the twenty-eighth-largest fund management company in the world.

Life insurance, for the first time, provided Ernest with a decent, middle-class income, and enabled him to escape the mean poverty of his childhood. He now could hobnob with business owners, bankers, and lawyers and judges. Among those he met was Harry Knight, the wealthy co-owner of Knight Brothers' lumber company, one of the biggest lumber firms in the British Empire (according to family lore). Mr. Knight, in turn, introduced Ernest to his niece, Miss Lynda Knight, sometime in 1909.

It did not take long for the couple to become serious about each other, even though most of their discourse was in writing. But write they did. Some days, Ernest fired off three letters! Lynda wrote less frequently, but sent several letters a week to Ernest, who was moving about rural Ontario selling insurance.

Thanks to frequent trains, letters between the two went back and forth at least daily, and sometimes three times a day. It was almost as good as email or Facebook today. Trains of that era often included a mail-sorting car, in which mail was picked up at each station and sorted for delivery at stations down the line. (One can visit such a mail-sorting car at the B&O Railway Museum, in Baltimore, Maryland.)

Ernest and Lynda's letters were written by fountain pen in neat, cursive handwriting. When I found the letters in Grandad's wooden box, the original blue ink had faded to brown. Ernest usually wrote on company or hotel stationery, while Lynda wrote on plain white notepaper. They were stamped by the location of origin and affixed with a penny stamp showing a portrait of King George V of England.

The meeting with Harry Knight was a fortuitous accident. The two men met in the King Edward Hotel in Burke Falls. In a letter a year later, on December 29, 1909, Ernest wrote, "My darling Lynnie, A year ago tonight the train leaving Burke Falls was late. The fact sealed your fate and mine. And how glad I am, how providential it seems to me… I cannot express." Two years after that date, he wrote,

> I was a long time accepting his [Uncle Harry's] invitation to Burke Falls but when I did I met someone who lured me back quite frequently. Five times in seven months... so going some!... Do you remember when I escorted you home from Uncle Harry's later that evening?... So you remember it?... I went back with purpose stronger than ever to come back some time—for you... Good night and pleasant dreams, Yours, Ernest.

Lynda Knight was worlds away from the innocent milkmaids of Derbyshire. She was well educated, well connected, an accomplished church musician and singer, and a photographer who developed and printed her own pictures in the darkroom. She was smart and she was beautiful—with dark hair and brilliant blue eyes.

Ernest and Lynda wrote to each other several times a day while Ernest was on the road selling insurance. That, of course, was most of the time. Their correspondence tells much about the young man's businesses life. Fortunately, most of their letters from 1909 to 1915 were present in Ernest's wooden trunk.

Ernest was usually on the road in the years between 1909 and 1915. He spent many lonely nights in hotels and boarding houses in small communities in Ontario. Commercial travellers like himself often rented hotel or boarding rooms for days and weeks at a time. Typically, the hotel lobby contained a table where the travelling men could sit down and write to their loved ones. (Nowadays, many hotels feature similar rooms with tables where travelling businesspeople plug in their laptops to the hotel Wi-Fi, explore the internet, and write.)

Ernest did not enjoy these cramped facilities and wrote to Lynda on November 5, 1910, from his room in the Hotel Cornwall in Sault Ste. Marie.

> This is a good hotel, but my room is cold and my hands can scarcely write and I do not care to go down to the commercial room to write to you... please address me as you used to, Ernest, as there are other Dawsons here. Lovingly yours, Ernest Dawson.

In another letter, dated March 20 the same year, he writes from Sudbury.

> My own Lynnie,... I am thinking of a curious phase of commercial life. Here I am at the writing table writing to my own with my

right elbow knocking the left of another commercial man who is writing. We are so close as to make it the easiest thing imaginable for me to read the other's yet although the table is crowded on all sides as this is, not one fears the others and I judge the majority are writing to their loves... Ever yours, Ernie.

By January 18, 1910, Ernest was quoting the Bible to Lynda.

"For whither thou goest I will go; and where thou lodgest I will lodge. Thy people shall be my people and thy God my God; whither thou diest I will die and there be buried, the Lord do so to me and more also, if but with part thee and me." Amen to this Lynda!

A year from their meeting, Ernest presented Lynda with a ring. She kept it quiet at first, but not for long. In an undated letter, she told Ernest,

I did not forget my ring as you feared. I thought afterwards that you would be wondering if I had. Mrs. Church (your favourite) was here for half an hour this morning. She spied my ring but hadn't the cheek to ask where it came from, which surprised me considerably. She had a look at it so it won't be long now till everybody in B.F. knows. So prepare yourself...

Ernest began another pattern when he availed himself of new technology in the company office in Sault St. Marie. He rightly predicted that Lynda would save his letter: "My Darling Girl—... The Stenographer is not writing this. I'm writing on my new machine myself [typewriter] and am writing on it as I can write faster and better than by hand... (I ought to keep a carbon copy of these letters but am not, for I am hoping I shall be able to see any of them fifty years from now if alive)."

By 1910, Ernest had begun to measure his progress in terms of his steady promotion in the insurance business, then marrying Lynda and settling down somewhere with her. In January 1910, he wrote to his future wife, describing an aggressive approach to his work:

My dear Lynda, ... At the best I imagine it will take me two years to get into condition financially before I may ask you to come... When I earn what I feel I shall be worth to a firm in two years experience I shall be able to provide a nice little home for you to hold sway in… Two years ago today I arrived in Campbellford to set up shop as District manager… A total stranger I had never before been in Campbellford and I did not know single soul in my territory. I had had less than two years' experience in the business, I soon found my feet and had a fairly good year. At the close of the year my territory was joined to that of Peterborough, giving me three and a half counties to look after… I have covered the large distance thoroughly in the year, gaining considerable experience in organization etc. Now I am wondering how the next two years will find me. Well au revoir Sweetheart and a fond good night,

Ernest

Ernest was not content with simply selling insurance. His competitive spirit showed up with his regular mention in company honours, such as the top ten monthly rankings and the annual "honour list" for sales. He also began writing for company and industry publications, often composing instructional and inspirational pieces aimed at other salesmen. He was obviously a good communicator, both on his feet and in writing. His picture often appeared in company magazines, along with his ranking among salesmen.

Lynda writes to him in April of 1912:

Saturday… your letter came as expected yesterday morning and oh, I was glad to get it… at 6 pm… Have read all the numerous little 'articles' in the Insurance Journal. You are getting some great boosts, aren't you?

Ernest was apparently a hot commodity in central Ontario. In 1910, he made a temporary job change, leaving the insurance industry for a position as the Knight Brothers' lumber company sales representative. He talked of "giving up what they call a 'cinch' to go to Burke Falls" and relayed the opinion of another insurance man who told him he had "not the slightest doubt of me making good."

The move to the Knight Brothers was a real switch for Ernest, largely motivated by a desire to be near Lynda. As he noted, the move required him to give up some of his independence. He had not, he wrote, had a 'boss' for four years and for the last two years I have had a managing position in my field. But I guess I can take orders yet if I have to. I suppose if I cannot I won't be much good... The Co. [Manufacturers' Life] is going to get me to train a man before I leave. I do not know what kind of 'success' he will make of it with only a month's training. The Head office will have to stay with him in the matter of training after I pass in my check.

As he considered his new position, he wrote in a Valentine's Day letter to Lynda his strong feelings about the insurance business, as both a salesman and a customer.

My insurance life is drawing to a close. I would not exchange the experience for $10,000. It's worth more than that to me... Do you know, I often think that insurance should help to check the mad rush for money when people feel that should death occur the families are safe and if they find they can provide a reasonable living and pay premiums. I feel quite right myself with guaranteed catch of six thousand at death ($1,000 of accident insurance). There will at least be enough to cover my debt and bury me, eh?

Eight months later, though, Ernest was no longer a full-time lumber agent. The experiment ended, apparently not well—he might have decided he was not making enough money. However, he probably longed for the independence of the agent's life too. He went back to insurance but combined this work with the lumber business. He wrote in September of his agreement with another large insurance company.

My dear Lynnie,... I have written to the Imperial [Life Insurance Company] saying I would be there on the sixth. They offer to pay my expenses. As so I am alright as far as their impression is concerned... I have virtually decided if they (The Imperial) will give me a hundred dollars a month and commission and other little points satisfactorily arranged, I will go to Sault St. Marie for them. I think they will give it me. I must have a hundred a month salary though. That will make you a little less fearful will it not?

Once back in the insurance business, Ernest quickly returned to high sales and success. By December of that year, he was tenth on Imperial Life's sales honour roll in November. He quickly insinuated himself into the business hierarchy of the Sault. He reported on his high-status associates to Lynda. Clearly, he had ambitions for the high life. This is also the first time he mentions mining as an interest.

> I dine this evening with the Lawyer of Lake Superior Corporation (a corporation capitalized in the hundreds of millions of dollars). I dined last evening with Lawyer P.T. Roland (son of one of Toronto's wealthiest men)... I am at least welcome to the place. Yesterday I had a couple of hours' chat (to say nothing of 50 cent cigars) with one of the Superior Corporation's officials, the Chief of Mines, a man who appears to know exactly what transportation and mining conditions are in every quarter of the globe, not excluding Superior district, a fine fellow drawing a salary close to $10,000 a year. I also had a long chat with the vice president, Mr. Taylor, an Englishman who at the present time is handling some fifteen millions of English capital... Mr. Ernst, a man who draws $10,000 a year for supplying technical information regarding the building of a six-million-dollar steel mill. All [these] figures will go to making my princely salary look small to you. Never mind, I have not yet met the person I would change places with if I had to do without you.

Lynda was impressed, writing back November 8 of that year,

> You are certainly hobnobbing with a pretty 'classy' bunch. I am very glad that you are meeting such nice people. Your salary still looks quite 'princely' to me, for a young fellow like you, although hardly of the proportions to admit of 'superb dinner' '50 cent cigars,' etc. However, some day we'll share them won't we? Yours lovingly, Lynda.

If $10,000 was a great yearly salary, what was Ernest making? In another letter he predicted that on a commission basis he was making practically $3,000 a year. A good, middle-class figure, probably enough to entertain married life at the time.

Sault Ste. Marie was a growing, high-energy city, where Ernest said there lived not one "old person." If they were old in years, he maintained, they were "youthful in spirit." He called the Sault a "young man's town." From his residence in the International Hotel, he threw himself energetically into the town's activities, making contacts in everything from football to the choral society.

Ernest also led a dual business life, maintaining his role with the Knight Brothers' lumber company at the same time as selling insurance. He told Lynda about this scheme in a November 23 letter.

> I came across a thing which I would not care to have the Imperial Life see, The Sault Express had a paragraph running something like this: "New firm come to town—Mr. A.E. Dawson a capable and energetic young man from Toronto has opened an office here for the Knight Bros of Burke Falls who cater to the building and lumber trade. Mr. Dawson will also devote some of his time in the interests of the Imperial Life etc. Etc." I haven't a copy of the paper or I would send you it. Rather amusing isn't it. "Some of my time"—the Imperial would say, yes the "sum of my time."...
> Good bye sweetheart your dear old boy, Ernest

Working these two jobs may have been Ernest's first serious business deception. I don't know what his dealings as a salesman were like but keeping his work for the Knight Brothers a secret from Imperial Life was a deception.

Ernest worried about his side operations for the Knight Brothers. "The Soo is a small place after all. I believe I now know most of those worth knowing. I'm known equally as K.B.'s agent as Imperial Life. I believe. It's a wonder that Imperial Life has not yet got wind of it. I am sure they would mention the fact in some way did they hear of my connection with the K.B. Co."

He worked hard in Sault Ste. Marie. He told Lynda, in the racist language of the times, "One has to work like a n--- though to make up a decent [living]. Some business in the K.B. line—I sent in another order for a car lot of stuff today." Later he records a large order from the Lake Superior Corporation (mentioned above) that included a large amount of white ash for a laboratory, the lumber to be felled and shipped from Burke Falls. "I don't know the estimated value of the job but I believe it quite a large sum."

He kept insurance work high on his agenda, however. In April 1911, he told his fiancée that he'd had his best month yet and had ranked on Imperial Life's Honour Roll for sales every month of the year. Only fifteen salesmen had been so reported, he said.

About this time, Ernest appears to have added speculation into his income sources. He was playing the stock market as well as indulging in land speculation a full decade before the general population began speculating in stock. In a February 1911 letter to Lynda, he describes a trip to Toronto connected with stock trading. He seems to have caught the gambler's excitement in stocks already, at a time when other more conservative Canadians were just beginning to play the market and buy insurance policies.

> Girlie mine,... One of my chief reasons for going to Toronto is to see if I can find a market for some shares I hold in a Canadian concern. 10 shares of par value 100.00 each. I think they are worth in total about $600.00 more but if there appears to be no immediate prospect of an advance in price I shall endeavor to sell them. Ask your dad if he does not want a good old Methodist gamble—it's oil—... The Colombian Oil and Gas Co. Ltd... some people who think they know the stock will go to 500.00. If it does, what I now hold as worth 600.00 will be worth $6000.00 OF COURSE IT'S A DREAM.

The letters never tell us whether the gamble paid off, but two weeks later, in March, Ernest confides that he will be cash poor at their projected wedding date, unless he can sell some land he's invested in. He had money tied up in several residential building lots. He asks her to decide on a wedding date based on his projected financial difficulties. Thus, even before they were married, Lynda has discovered that her fiancé was a gambler at heart, a gambler who dealt in high stakes. He wrote:

> June it shall be if you say so... I shall be pretty "hard up" if I cannot dispose of my lots or some of them to advantage before that time... We shall have more than fifteen dollars, though it may be bid up in property. I have some extra heavy payments on property to make about June and July and although I am not over anxious as to my being able to engineer them one way or another,

> there is a possibility of contingencies arising, such as the non sale of property in the meantime, to meet these at the drop in values etc.... June and July will be crucial months with me. I fully expect to pass through easily... Your own Ernest

Even the life insurance business was plagued by uncertainty. He complained on another day that insurance business "plays with me very much as a youngster plays with a shuttlecock." This was a day with applications for $15,000 in coverage in in one day. "I rarely count my chickens before they are hatched but they appear so much in the egg... I shall tell you of a fairly large brood."

Lynda decided on a June wedding despite Ernest's financial uncertainties. They did not have a honeymoon, however.

In May, a month before his wedding, Ernest reflected on his rapid rise in fortune since arriving in Canada.

> Six years ago today I stepped off the good ship Vancouver at Quebec, and now, today, you are off to Toronto to buy your wedding frocks in which to marry that young-looking man... who landed, unharmed and uncaring into a vast territory and amid a thousand varying influences... just six years ago today. On that day, had you asked me, I imagine there would have been very little in me to interest you and I, I was not in the word... forseeing [sic]... fortunes.

Ernest took his bride to a modest home in Sault Ste. Marie. The correspondence ends there, since they now lived together, except for a period of a year or so when Ernest was sent to establish the company in Saskatchewan. There he pioneered automobile use (see next chapter), and thus began a serious interest in insuring cars. This interest was to play an important role in the next phase of his business life.

By the end of the decade, he was promoted to become the manager of the prestigious Central Ontario Branch for Imperial Life. He was a successful company man, making a very good living. I believe he became a wealthy man during this period. He also became an eminent man in the region—socializing with bank managers and judges, and he established his young family in the community.

The key to Ernest's success as an insurance agent was probably summed up in a speech he made to the Toronto insurance industry.[3] He made a rather startling suggestion at the time—that personality and psychology determined an agent's success, not "the numbers" of the insurance policy. Two publications recorded his remarks:

> Personality is the chief stock-in-trade of the men charged with selling life or any other kind of insurance, according to A.E. Dawson, manager of the Central Ontario Branch of the Imperial Life Assurance Company, who recently addressed the Toronto Life Underwriters' Association. Basing his remarks on the subject, "My Ideal Insurance Agent," Mr. Dawson pointed out that while the agent might be serving a good company, with policies equal to any, he recognizes that the real thing that enables him to get business in face of competition offering equal security and benefits is to add to his company's benefits a superior personality. The equality of personality, continued Mr. Dawson, must be fully felt from within not impressed from without.
>
> While difficult to define, it was yet capable of being developed by the individual. The ideal agent ever strives to excel in his business. He also strives at a fine and subtle distribution of manner and dress. He allows himself to slip into the local manner of talking, appreciating the fact and a precise cultivation of speech, preciseness of thinking. His sentences are well-rounded and his manner of utterance has an air of finality from which there seems to be no appeal.

Reading this account of Ernest's views on salesmanship, one thinks back to the ways he effectively absorbed himself into the rural life of Derbyshire. Ernest had clearly learned to be an effective persuader, using a collection of tools at his disposal… dress, an air of authority, and an understanding of the

---

3   *The Financial Post*, "The Ideal Agent Does Not Appeal By Logic Alone, No Life Policy Sold on Basis of Strict Mathematics, Strive To Excel, Personality Insurance Agent's Chief Stock-in-Trade—Makes It Possible to Get Business in Face Keen Competition," year unknown.

psychological needs of his potential customers. These persuasive skills were to serve him well for many years.

The speech went on to describe the necessary mental discipline needed to be an effective salesman.

> Life insurance men, notwithstanding their variety, divide into two classes. One class embraces those in whom the highness of the business of life insurance has made a deep and profound impression and who realizes that however alert and watchful they may be can never become bigger than the institution they represent. The other class is formed of those whose mentality has become dwarfed by the immensity of the business. They have ceased to think of the institution and think only of the work at hand. Day by day—week after week, and year after year they follow the line of least resistance. While many of these latter can talk of nothing but insurance, their talk is of the insignificant details and with many too, while they may be quite large writers, their grade of service is not high nor is it at all complete. The "ideal" agent first of all appreciates they fact that there are limits to the benefits which his company can offer at the price. He also recognizes that there are limits to the benefits that the company can offer him as a representative. As a consequence he starts out satisfied—satisfied with his company, satisfied with his company's policies and satisfied with his job. Mr. Dawson continued as follows:

Then is he not merely satisfied with his job, but he has pride in his work. And well he may. He never ceases to marvel at the miraculous possibilities of the insurance idea. I like to roll it over and over in my mind and contemplate it in my mind as it will advance by geometrical progression during the next generation or two. We may well nerve his arm. My hero is not so perfect as to be without his blue funks—his depressing days and occasional hopeless nights—because he's human, but he doesn't quit the moment he becomes down-hearted. I wonder how many men have quit on the eve of success. Thousands probably. I have had men come in and lay down their rate book and supplies—disheartened and discouraged. Unable to prevail upon them I have had to let them go their own sweet way—and have felt sure that another effort or two would have carried them over the top. Now although he is conscious of purpose and does not quit, he knows enough to lay off temporarily when stale. When this happens he betakes himself to his hobby and forgets for a time his part in the program.

After a breathing spell, he comes back to earth—invigorated and ready for good work. Had he continued while stale, he might easily have spoiled some good prospects. It's just possible some other agent has cleaned up a mess or two of his, but he accepts this as the fortunes of war, and accepts the other man's right to live and prosper.

By 1920, Ernest was ready for his next step—moving to Toronto, and investing in and managing a new Canadian insurance company.

The Great Wheelbarrow Race

Ernest Dawson, for all his stern demeanour with his grandchildren, loved fun, loved risk, and loved to gamble. He was comfortable finding himself "on the edge" —where success and failure lay on either side of his endeavour. These qualities played a major role in his later involvement with the stock market and investing.

Ernest loved nothing more than a good bet…with stakes as low as a few matchsticks (games with his wife in old age) to an island vacation home. He won the vacation home in Lake of the Woods during a bridge game. The family enjoyed the island for several years and his children had pleasant memories of swimming, boating, and general fun on the island. In another bridge game, however, Ernest lost the island. The luck of the draw, he might have explained to his disappointed family.

Betting made life interesting for Ernest. During the teens and the 1920s, his circle of friends included many prominent citizens of Peterborough[4] and Toronto. In this undated memoir, written years later in prison,[5] he describes a widely reported betting adventure with a group of those eminent citizens. They happened to be his bridge group—Ernest played bridge regularly most of his life. This event took place on June 15, 1922. It was during the time he had become vice president and general manager of his new venture, Toronto Casualty, Marine, and Fire Insurance Company. In the account, Ernest appears pleased with his eminent status in the community, and with the wide publicity given to his adventure.

The Upholstered Wheelbarrow

The bet arose at a game of bridge. The road from Lakefield to Peterboro had been newly gravelled to a depth of several inches and in some manner now forgotten the question had arisen whether or not the gravel having been laid on thick was really any improvement then or later and Jack Strickland laughed! [He] was one of the bridge foursome who objected, in that when the gravel had been worn...the road would be very much better than it had been.

The argument became hot and heavy. The others at the leading table were E.P Tate, the village J.P., and G.G. Connall the manager of the local branch of the Royal Bank.

By some means, also forgotten, the argument developed into a [bet],...taking the view that it would impede traffic and be just a total loss and the expense wasted. Strickland and Tate bet a sum of money, the amount of which we each agreed...to divide... that they could push me to Peterboro, a distance of just about ten miles within the time I had stated...five hours. [Earnest bet they could

---

4   Note that Peterborough, Ontario, the modern spelling, is spelled Peterboro in the account. The village of Lakefield, now a resort town on the Trent-Severn Waterway, is about ten miles north from the city of Peterborough. It was home for the Dawson family for many years.

5   Dawson, A.E., Jail Notes, page 118.

not.] Connall was the umpire and would drive in his car as we proceeded and divide any points of dispute which might arise and be in Peterboro to drive us back.

It was agreed that the task should take place of the next holiday, 1 July, when all hands would be free to devote the time required. I was to be allowed to take a book to read and an umbrella to keep the sun off me.

We were all well known in the district and the news got abroad that a fabulous sum had been wagered on the event and day by day the rumoured amount grew and interest increased until at noon on the day assigned a crowd, hundreds strong, had assembled at the village Town Hall—the starting point—to see us off. I had taken my garden wheelbarrow down to the local harness maker and had it... upholstered and told the old man in charge to withhold his bill until I told him whom to charge it to. If I lost I was bound not to have to pay also for the trimmings.

I was driven down to the Town Hall and waited to sit in the barrow carrying a large unabridged international dictionary... and weighing nearly forty pounds. As I sat there with my umbrella secured above me, the two pushers appealed to the umpire and the book was disallowed.

We started off at noon, each of us having had an early lunch. The lunch was very nearly my undoing for before the first half mile was traversed I was so uncomfortable that I almost yielded my wager—but presently I became more easy in the stomach and more comfortable about the depth of gravel through which the wheelbarrow was being pushed. It seemed to me impossible that the pushers should be able to last out the course.

Connall had brought refreshments with which he kept the working party in good spirits, but deprived it to me on the grounds of my being the wagerer. I should have known better than to agree to Connall as umpire and this mistake was confirmed when after having gone some two miles on the way he agreed to a request that one of the pushers be allowed to fasten a strap to the front of the barrow and pull while the other pushed. I objected to this but Connall overruled the objection.....and the frequent stops for refreshment afforded...damages as the road was active with cars from Lakefield following us on the course and cars meeting us on the way from Peterboro, most of them having no other surface than to wait the event.

Because I seldom drank, and in any event was deprived of any share of the refreshments under the ruling of the umpire, I had a sneaking hope that someone might lay a charge of drinking on the highway or carrying open bottles of liquor in an automobile—by this time I included the umpire in the list of those against whom I felt aggrieved.

For a considerable part of the journey, the edge of the road was free of gravel, it being the technique of road runners that traffic would gradually push the gravel out as far as the edge of the road. Advantage was taken of every bit of bare road and my protestations went unheard by Connall who had felt the need of frequent stimulation as much as the "pushers" and had... the resistance necessary to me, who was driving a motor vehicle on a public highway. He became more and more prejudiced [favouring] the Pushers as we proceeded and invariably ruled in favour of the Pushers.

Before we had reached the halfway mark of the race... a car met us with photographers and a reporter from the Peterboro Examiner whom they sent out to mark our progress... This had the effect of stimulating interest in Peterboro and before our arrival there, crowds had gathered on both sides of the street. The corner of George and Hamilton Streets was our objective and as we swung on to the main thoroughfare it was evident that much of the holidaying city had turned out.

The two pushers were well known and a lot of ragging came from the sidelines. Pete, who was a most correct Englishman, one who never before, with few exceptions, had been seen in his braces, now lead the parade, his coat and vest off and thrown in Cannall's car and bending slightly forward thus pulling the strap over his shoulder, looked little like the dignified and careful Justice of the Peace known to many of the inhabitants.

Strickland was at the controls of the wheelbarrow—also minus coat and vest—and both had stood the rather gruelling ten miles surprisingly well and we went forward at a fast pace. All traffic had been stopped, even the streetcars were lined up beyond Hunter Street where the crowd filled the middle of the road. A resounding cheer went up as they turned towards the Hunter Street curb and let me out.

They had won by over an hour.

The Associated Press had the story from the Examiner and during the months that followed I received press clippings from friends in Seattle to... Cleveland and others far away.

One such friend wrote from Cleveland,[6] "...the whole uncivilized world was shaken by the announcement of the Associated Press that you were wheelbarrowed by Strickland and Tate from Lakefield to Peterborough for a wager...the nature of the wager was not given and there is great curiosity here and in England, especially to have the mystery solved...a widespread public concern the facts should be made known..."

---

6   Ritchie, Ryerson, Letter, June 28, 1922.

Leslie Y. Dawson

A.E. Dawson at the helm of his wheelbarrow.

CHAPTER 6:
Married Life and Success in Business

Even before they married, Ernest and Lynda had begun a long lifetime of separations. Ernest was continually on the road, selling insurance and Knight Brothers' lumber. In later years, as an insurance and securities executive, he was frequently away on business travel, or living weekdays in his exclusive Toronto men's club, the Hunt Club. Lynda kept busy at home as a piano teacher and church choir director and pianist. During their courtship in 1910, she describes one of their many partings.

> I cannot write a very long letter this time as this is a very busy day for me. I have given two lessons since dinner and have five more to give today... I am beginning to realize that you have gone; at least I began to realize it this morning at the Union Station. If you had said a single word about parting I'd have given the people in the car an 'exhibition' not of temper but of tears. I think you knew it and very wisely refrained from saying anything. Your loving Lynda.

In another letter, she wished, fervently, that Ernest's many absences were not a portent of the future.

Lynda tried to keep up with Ernest's movements and activities. On November 6, 1910, before their marriage, she wrote,

> I am very glad too that you are favourably impressed with Sudbury and the Soo, especially the latter of course. So it has 14000

inhabitants. I have read parts of each of the first two letters to dad and Laura [her sister] and dad was particularly struck with the 14000. He kept saying "Phew! 14000." It must be a musical town too, or they wouldn't be attempting the Messiah nor would they be having the Professor as the organist. Goodbye, your own Lynda.

Lynda led a hectic life in Burke Falls, but by late 1910 she was preoccupied with her growing romance with Ernest. She wrote, in an undated letter,

My dear Boy, All day Thursday I was at the piano, practicing my two hours in the morning and teaching from one o'clock in the afternoon... until choir practice time 8:45. We practiced until ten o'clock at the church then... It seems tonight as though I would be willing to live in the Arctic Regions or in the South Sea Islands only to be with you and to feel your arms around me and to lay my head on your shoulder. Who would have imagined that practical Lynda Knight would ever have admitted as much to any man living? Not I. Good night dear, Lynda.

Later, in December of that year, Lynda told Ernest that she was cutting back on her student load to a mere twenty. Before then she had thirty-two students.

Lynda wrote of daily events in Burke Falls. On November 20, 1910, she penned this account.

My dear Ernest, You would be surprised if you could see me tonight. I am sitting at the sewing room table, writing under difficulties, as the only light I have is an old coal oil lamp. And what is more, it is all I hope to have for the next few days, as the dynamo burned out last night and dad has to take part of the machinery to Toronto tomorrow. About eight o'clock last night the lights here suddenly went out, the result of a belt breaking on one of the dynamos. All the current suddenly being left on the other dynamo burned it out. The belt was quite easily fixed and tonight lights in all the churches were on, but the other machine is pretty well 'on the brink' and will be until dad gets home from Toronto... Mrs. Lamb said, 'It isn't very nice sitting in the dark is it?' She said 'It's alright Lynda if you are sitting with the right person.' I said, 'But what if you haven't got the right person?' Her answer wasn't very nice. She said, 'Take the next best.' But as the next best doesn't exist with me I came home to write to the 'best.' As ever, Your loving Lynda

In 1920 the couple began to get down to the practicalities of life together. Ernest wrote, "Lynnie girl, have just totaled up my month's work. I find on a commission basis it amounts to $243.18—out of which I have rec. $100 salary,... Practically $3000 per year. Think you can live on that?... I thought these figures might interest you. Do they? A.E.D."

Lynda was impressed. She responded,

> Dear Old Boy,... I was very glad to hear of your very successful month's work. The Company must be very much pleased. You speak of earning $243 'on a commission Basis' I understand. You get your salary now and at the end of a certain time whatever business you did over the average of $100 a month. Anyway I knew you are 'making good' and that the company will be well pleased and that is the main consideration with me. Yes, I think I could live very nicely of the amount per year that you mentioned, or a much smaller sum if necessary.

Ernest also began to look at his personal finances more closely. He gave up one luxury with this in mind, writing in January of 1910,

> My dear Lynda, I have suddenly come to the conclusion that I cannot afford the Mendelssohn Choir this year. I told Edgar [Ted, Lynda's brother] in my letter last night I was going but it is expensive to go... as much as I would like it. I need the necessary cash for much more important things. I have never subjected myself to very much economy and I felt it would be a good time to commence right away, for I've certainly got to do it soon or I shall never have that little cottage with its cosy corners and open fireplace... Ever yours, Ernest

Lynda wanted to be consulted when Ernest considered changes in his business life. She wrote,

> Dear Boy, You do not know how glad I was when I opened your letter this morning and found that you were not going to resign your position with the Imperial. Of course, I would not have wanted you to stay with them under conditions such as you hinted of in your letter yesterday, but I am glad that you need not make another change just now. It was very good of you to let me know... don't think you will ever have cause to chide me for 'butting in' with your business affairs so long as I am not kept in ignorance when there is a crisis or a big change in view or something like that... Lovingly yours, Lynda

As their marriage approached, it appeared that Ernest would be working out of Sault Ste. Marie. He looked back on the immense changes in his fortunes since arriving in Canada in 1905. Again, he could not help boasting of his success and wrote to his sweetheart,

> I left her [England] behind, came to Canada and found a new and larger sphere yet broader to view... (perhaps a greater value for the dollar, I don't know!)... but anyway, as the summer of 1910 approaches, of nearly five years in Canada I have—You! I wonder how you can be content to become the wife of a person whom not a soul in Canada knew of five years ago. A fellow who believes in no other pedigree than honest parents and failing even that, it matters little to the fellow, eh?

Ernest set about finding housing appropriate for their married life.

> Mrs. Broughton is right concerning houses here, they are frightfully high. One cannot afford to pay the rent. It's cheaper to buy, even at the inflated prices asked. I was negotiating for one this week, a house the owners are asking $4000.00 for which would not be worth much more than H.K.'s house in B.F If... I buy I shall rent it out till Oct. Then I suppose live in it until I can build.

Ernest dreamed of the marriage, but meanwhile led a full social life in the Soo. He was involved in the church, sports, and cultural activities. On November 22 of 1910, he wrote from the International Hotel.

Dear Girlie,... around Oct 2nd next... here will no longer be Lynda Knight, though she may be Lynda Knight Dawson if she wishes... I don't think I told you of the football match to come off on Saturday in which I play. The auditors are an enthusiastic bunch and we are playing the high school chaps. I expect we will get licked pretty heartily for not one of our side has kicked a ball in years and as for our wind, well it's nonexistent... Also there's a business man's proposition to form a choral society and pay Clapperton a salary as conductor. They propose to make me Secretary, without a salary I presume. Must be on account of my musical ability... Your affectionate boy, Ernest

Ernest pictured a very traditional, but enlightened, relationship with his future wife. His views, today, strike me as incredibly sexist and condescending, but for the time he was probably quite progressive. Men and women lived defined roles, with few exceptions. On December 6, 1910, he wrote,

Your ideas are ever practical and worthy of consideration and for that fact I have often congratulated myself upon the possession of a very sensible little woman for a future wife, one who does not put with a long string of ideas at once foolish and out of the question, but one who has no lack of ideas, but before giving voice to any of them gives them practical thought and common-sense reasoning with the result that when one is brought forth it is listened to with respect. That is what I like—always in a woman's sphere, that is; I do not like women who interfere with business, suggesting things of which she has no actual knowledge of conditions and about which she cannot hope to give any capable advice or upon which she is not expected to be able to give any intelligent comment, as her husband is supposed to know his business and she hers... This however is needless to you, for I think your feelings are of this nature too, and need no suggestions from me for instance on how you should lay the cloth or make the beds or dust the furniture.

In another letter, he added,

I would not make of you a goddess here, but a wife, who would be with me here as a mortal, she could share my joy and laughter,

> my sorrows, and... a joy doing either... One who would need my care, protection, and thought, and to share my purse, my food, my home. So Lynnie darling, are you still willing?

Sometime in 1910, Lynda began to correspond with Ernest's father and sisters. Distance and time had mellowed Ernest's feelings about his father. Lynda told Ernest that she was pleased with the letters and planned to continue. Ernest was also pleased.

> As for Father's liking you, he can't help it. You are made of the stuff he admires, candid, thoughtful, and kind. The thought of you will cheer his old days and heaven only knows he deserves a happy life from now on. His life up to the present has been as full of care, sometimes misfortunes, truly the rain fallen on the just and the unjust.

The couple was married in 1911, and a year later Lynda gave birth to the first of their six children, Harry. She gave birth to the five others and learned the rigours of raising a family with an absentee father.

In 1912, Ernest was sent west to manage the new Saskatchewan branch of Imperial Life. He spent a year there, with Lynda raising babies alone in the east. By the end of the decade Ernest was promoted to become the manager of the prestigious Central Ontario Branch for Imperial Life. He was a successful company man, making a very good living with less travel. I believe he became a wealthy man during this period. He also became an eminent person in the region.

I can only guess at Ernest and Lynda's relationship during these years. Because they no longer needed to write to each other, we have only anecdotal stories of the time from their now-deceased children. They lived in a series of homes in Peterborough, Lakefield, and eventually in Toronto's wealthy Rosedale neighbourhood. They spent summers at an island vacation home in a lake (acquired through Ernest's bet in a bridge game, and subsequently lost the same way). The family sailed, swam, and explored this idyllic location. The boys attended a posh boarding school, Lakefield, where they acquired the classical education and values their father had dreamed of for them. Today, the same school is attended by the world' elite, even royalty.

Ernest's ideas on a good school are reflected in his unpublished novel, *In the Shadow of Orkis*. The idealized school, Orkis, he describes in the novel sounds much like the Lakefield school his children attended. He also describes, in one of his early letters to Lynda, the demeanour of a group of boarding school children he met in his travels. He was greatly impressed by their discipline and intelligence, and told Lynda that he hoped their children might attend such a school some day.

The Dawsons soon became well-to-do citizens, first of Peterborough and then Toronto. Life was good. Ernest had left the hopelessness of England far behind, but not his overriding ambition. He had much more to do, much more to accomplish.

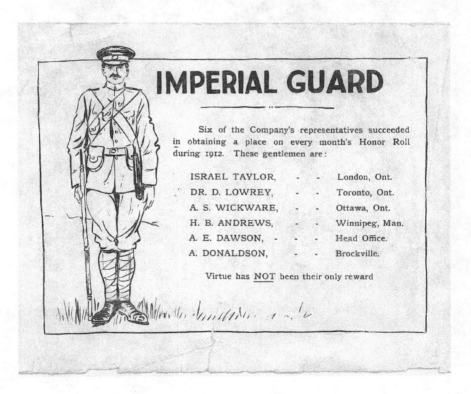

A.E. Dawson was frequently listed as a top insurance salesman for Imperial Life.

A.E. Dawson began his family during the 1910s.

Lynda Knight, shown here with first sons, Allen (left) and Harry.

A.E. Dawson's youngest son, Don, with the family dog, Moodie. After his father died, Don collected and organized his father's records and writings in the old wooden trunk.

A.E. Dawson and Lynda Knight Dawson with their family in the late 1910s. Shown here are Harry (far left), Barbara (on Lynda's knee), Don, Ken, and Allen (far right). Darrel had not yet been born.

A.E. Dawson made his way into Toronto's elite, as shown here by his acceptance into the Toronto Hunt club.

Leslie Y. Dawson

Lizzie, the First Car

Ernest always stood at the forefront of new technology when it came to typewriters, telephones, or, as here, automobiles. What follows is the memoir, written in his Jail Notes, where he wrote about his first automobile, Lizzie. He acquired this car while working in Saskatchewan during the 1910s. This experience established Ernest's lifelong, happy relationship with automobiles. In his good years, he proudly bought a new Buick home every fall. He went on to pioneer Toronto Casualty's automobile insurance policies and to become the lead Canadian automobile insurance provider.

The anecdote also describes Ernest's chance encounter with an encampment of Aboriginal people, still living a traditional lifestyle on the prairies. Ernest is clearly fearful of the group, especially since he burst in on them so abruptly and destructively. At the time, the Riel Rebellion was within living memory, as was the Aboriginal victory in the Battle of Little Bighorn. By the time of this story, thousands of Aboriginal children were enrolled in residential schools, where they were treated as dangerous, uncivilized savages. This incident may well have been the first time this particular Aboriginal group had seen a car, and it was not a positive introduction by any means. It's interesting that Ernest felt no need to stop and apologize to the group.

The episode here also illustrates Ernest's penchant for taking risks and trying new things. We now call people like him "early adopters." He and Lynda were among the first to use such technologies as typewriters, international long-distance telephone service, and darkroom technology. Ernest had an abundance of self-confidence and was not averse to living on the edge. It apparently did not faze him to launch into the wilderness alone, with only rudimentary experience with the automobile. Did he even know if he had enough fuel to reach his destination and return?

I wondered, as I read this account, if Ernest was a brave man, a gambler, or a fool? Most likely he was all of the above.

Lizzie: My First Love

In 1912 when I was manager of the Saskatchewan Branch of the Imperial Life, I wrote head office suggesting I be furnished with a car to facilitate my movement about that Province. Cars had not yet become generally in use as may be [suggested] by the fact that my suggestion was held up in Toronto until it could be submitted to the Board of Directors! Today the company would have a dozen regional managers… whose authority would include such a decision. I believe mine was the first automobile to be purchased by the company. It was a Ford and [when it arrived] I was out on the wide prairie to learn to drive it.

Some weeks later when I had mastered the use of this revolutionary instrument, I decided to take a trip to a far point in the Southwest where it was proposed that a railway divisional train would be located.

I knew nothing of the roads down there except that it was fairly level prairies type of country for the most part with some rolling hills towards the end of my journey. I believe that there about my car was the first to be seen after I had reached a point. I forget the name of the place but it was a little more than a hundred miles…

I was alone in the car and after I had left Regina the land became mostly a prairie trail used by wagons and a rain had made the surface muddy and slippery, and when I reached the rolling country I would have to approach any moderate rise with a burst of speed to prevent slipping down before reaching the top. On one such rise, a little more steep than any I had encountered, the road went up the hill slantwise diagonally towards the top with the result that the car on the right hand side was at the disadvantage of being lop-sided, leaving some six or seven inches higher than on the left side.

Had I been a little more expert in driving, and had the surface been less slippery, I might have [made it to] the top of this short but rather sharp rise more successfully; as it was I became a little panicky and pushed the foot pedal into low gear which slowed down the car, then I [engaged] the hand throttle which sent the wheels rising. My whole attention was concentrated upon navigating the car to the top and I suddenly found good traction provided by the dry at the top and I found myself flying through an Indian encampment and scattered a ring of frightened ponies in any direction.

I saw the Indians jump up in dozens and looking almost as frightened as I felt. I put on another burst of speed and went down the other side of the hill and ran up the other side left the encampment, me scaring the scattered ponies falling about their hobbles in every direction. I made a careful note to try and find another way home as I did not want to again encounter this tribe for obvious reasons. I had topped the next rise and slid a slippery... and ran the car axle deep... and there I stood. I was not more than five or six hundred yards beyond the Indian encampment but fortunately was out of sight unless some of them had decided to come after me. I was in a fear of anxiety as I tried to move forward and backward and make a track by which I could rush the car out of the slough.

Frequently I stalled the engine and as frequently I had to get out and crank (There were no self-starters in those times) and each time I looked back up the hill with apprehension and wished devoutly that the engine would start up with less noise...

My next trouble was a boiling radiator. I was aware that the Indians in Southern Saskatchewan were regarded as friendly but my imagination made me question if this particular tribe was included in that regard, and even if I could be sure of that, how was I to know if even a friendly tribe would... in the face of an entirely new and strange, rattling, self-propelled vehicle which came suddenly upon them, scattering their ponies and almost knocking down their tepees, and so suddenly departing!

There was nothing for it but to let the car cool. For more than an hour I devoted my attention... on the hilltop behind me and forcing [it] back and forth until I roared out of it and up the next rise and away.

Swindler

I have had many cars since that date but I shall not likely forget Lizzy, my first love!

CHAPTER 7:
The 1920s and The Toronto Casualty Years

At the age of thirty-four, in 1921, Ernest Dawson launched a remarkable career as one of Canada's most prominent corporate leaders and financiers. With eleven other associates, he founded the Toronto Casualty Fire and Marine Insurance Company, an Ontario-based firm. Together the men bankrolled the infant insurance company, and stockholders put up the substantial assets necessary to ensure its financial health and its ability to meet claims. To invest as one of those shareholders, Ernest had to have accumulated substantial wealth himself.

Certainly, in 1921, the insurance industry looked like a good investment. During that year, Canadians bought an amount of insurance equalling the national post-war debt. Insurance looked good to Canadian consumers and to investors alike.

This chapter reflects information I found in newspapers and magazines published during the 1920s. Ernest's wooden trunk held very few materials about his business life during that decade or subsequent decades. Thus, the reader must pardon me for having to paint an inferred picture of Ernest's role in the industry, as suggested by articles on the front pages and financial columns in the *Globe and Mail*, the *Toronto Star*, and other periodicals. The story reflects my best guesses at what was going on and I offer apologies for any shortcomings. I also apologize for the rather dry, corporate history here... if you are not a corporate history wonk, it may come across as rather dull.

A Privately Launched Company

Toronto Casualty was probably a privately held company at first, in which a small group of shareholders controlled all the shares. The shares were not sold publicly at the time of incorporation. I have been unable to determine when the company went public. While the company may not have enjoyed as much capital as a publicly held company, the share values would be more stable and would be based on the actual value and assets of the company, not on investment trends in the market.

Elected in 1922, Ernest served as general manager and vice president of Toronto Casualty for eight years. Newspapers quoted him—as an apparently trusted source—more often than any other officer of the company.

Toronto Casualty took the Canadian insurance industry by storm, offering a five-dollar stock dividend at its second annual meeting on February 12, 1923. (Alas, I do not have any data on actual stock value.) The company rapidly became the pre-eminent Canada-based casualty insurance company in the country.

A New Adventure: Casualty Insurance

Ernest spent a good part of the 1910s selling and promoting life insurance. With Toronto Casualty, however, he entered a new field.

Casualty insurance covers losses in such events as accidents, liability lawsuits, theft, fire, and marine disasters. The casualty industry began in Britain during the 1840s, when Railway Passenger Assurance Company of Britain began to cover losses due to numerous railway accidents.[7] Insurers also went on to cover employers' liability during the 1880s. At that time agricultural workers began to sue their employers for liability after work-related accidents, especially accidents involving steam-powered threshing machines.

Casualty insurance presented more of a risk-taking venture than life insurance, which bases its premiums on reliable, predictable population death statistics. Casualty insurance must assess, instead, the relatively unpredictable risks associated with disasters, including large-scale catastrophes (such as storms and fires) and big financial losses (such as theft and robbery). Casualty

---

7 Young, Peter, *A Premium Business, A History of General Accident*, 1999. Page 11.

insurance is not for the faint of heart, and the industry was still establishing risks and premiums for many niche markets at the time.

Nobody ever accused Ernest of being faint-hearted, so it was not surprising to see him jump wholeheartedly into casualty insurance.

In the late 1800s and early 1900s, casualty insurance companies explored the financial possibilities of insuring many specialty niche areas. This included theft, livestock insurance (loss of animal herds due to disease, theft, natural disaster, etc.), plate-glass accidents, marine disasters, and eventually automobile accident insurance.

Toronto Casualty was established as a general casualty insurer, as "fire and marine" in its title indicated. It also took on automobile insurance right away. By 1925, the company had taken the lead among Canadian insurers for automobile insurance.[8]

A typical advertisement[9] for Toronto Casualty appeared in the *Ottawa Journal* in 1925. In the ad, the company stated that it covered losses from "any cause whatsoever," including burglary, fire, tempest, larceny, lightning, storm, theft, earthquake and flood. Even loss of luggage while travelling or pipes bursting were covered, as were losses from highway robbery, hold-ups, cheque alteration, forgery, and personal liability. "A Householder's Comprehensive Policy," the ad stated.

Big Name in Insurance and Investment

During the twenties, Ernest rapidly became a well-known public figure in the Toronto business world, juggling positions in a number of insurance and financial companies. The family eventually moved from their small-town home in central Ontario to the prestigious Toronto neighbourhood of Rosedale.

At home, Lynda threw herself into directing choral music in Toronto. Her girls' choir was featured with Sir Ernest MacMillan's famous Mendelssohn Choir in Toronto. The boys attended the prestigious private boarding school The Grove, later to become Lakefield College School in Lakefield, Ontario.

---

8 *The Ottawa Journal,* "Further Consolidation in Canadian Fire Insurance Organization, Control of Merchants and Employers Insurance Company of Montreal Secured by Toronto Casualty Group, Operations to be Extended All Over Canada, Oct. 12, 1925.
9 *The Ottawa Journal,* Advertisement, August 14, 1925.

(Today, Lakefield is probably Canada's pre-eminent private school.) Ernest's son Don, my father, recalled with pride that Ernest bought a new Buick every fall, and every fall he proudly drove the boys to Lakefield in his new car at the beginning of the term.

This was the portrait of A.E. Dawson frequently used in magazine and newspaper articles.

Swindler

Toronto Casualty occupied a large office on in downtown Toronto.

The Toronto Casualty staff, during the 1920s. A.E. Dawson, General Manager, sits forth from the left, bottom row.

Securities: A New Skill

In addition to running a new, ambitious insurance company, Ernest began to deal with investments. Of course, as general manager, he had to be familiar with investing Toronto Casualty's assets and profits in the securities and bond markets. He also appeared to play securities with his own investment companies on the side.

Ernest was cited and quoted in the *Globe and Mail* in various corporate capacities. He was the most frequently quoted spokesperson for Toronto Casualty. In 1925, *Maclean's* magazine featured a glowing, full-length biography (quoted in earlier chapters). He also was cited with other companies. For instance, he was president and general manager of the Canadian Associate Companies Limited, Investment Bankers. This was one of his first corporate forays into the securities industry and may have had to do with investing Toronto Casualty's asset capital. He also served on the board of Traders Finance Corporation in 1925, and in some capacity in the Ackerman-Dawson Company. We do not know the nature of the Ackerman-Dawson Company, but it was a big operation—it later bought out a major insurance company. All of these positions point to Ernest's activity in the securities industry, in addition to the insurance world.

Sometime during the early 1920s Ernest also formed the long-standing A.E. Dawson & Company, a securities firm that eventually specialized in mining stocks during the 1930s. One advertisement during the 1930s stated that A.E. Dawson & Company had joined the Toronto Stock Exchange (TSX) in 1925. Seat prices in the TSX's Standard Stock and Mining Exchange that year were $2,000 to $5,000 by that time, small potatoes for Ernest.

During the 1920s, Canadians were beginning to take risks in volatile mining and oil stocks. It was a form of gambling that offered the remote prospects of making it big, with little or no guarantee of success. It is probable that Ernest was involved in these stocks too, since he eventually specialized in the field.

Huge numbers of Canadians also began buying stocks on the margin. With stock prices going up continuously, it actually made sense to take out a loan, using existing stocks as collateral, and, in turn, use the loan to buy yet more stock. This made sense as long as the profits from sales exceeded interest rates—and, as long as stocks continued to go up in value. Since margin buying was so pervasive during the twenties, it would be surprising if Ernest were not doing it too, although I have no direct evidence of this.

The Dawson name was associated with a whirlwind of corporate buyouts, mergers, and big corporate deals. For instance, in 1923 the Ackerman-Dawson Company bought out the General Animals Insurance Co. of Montreal, a company that insured livestock, automobiles, and plate glass. General Animals was renamed the Canadian General Insurance Company, bringing its head office to Toronto. By 1929 the company claimed assets in excess of a million dollars and was transacting "very substantial business."[10]

Ernest and his associates created a close affiliation of several insurance companies called "the Toronto Casualty Group." The group included Toronto Casualty, Canadian General Insurance, Manufacturer's and Employers Guarantee, and others. This rather incestuous collection of firms shared risk and investments throughout the casualty insurance industry. In 1929, for instance, the Traders Finance Corporation, another member of the group, underwrote all of the Ford Motor dealerships throughout Canada. The newspaper article[11] reporting the General Animals deal noted the involvement of Toronto Casualty. The writer said, "The sound growth and steady development of the Toronto Casualty Co., will be a source of satisfaction to the numerous shareholders in this district."

Toronto Casualty thrived throughout the decade. On January 11, 1926, the Ontario Superintendent of Insurance, R. Leighton Foster (a frequently quoted national insurance regulator), wrote to Ernest. He said, "I also have a copy of your financial statement as at 31st December 1925. I am sure that you have reason to congratulate yourself upon your progress during the past year."

Automobile Insurance Innovator

During the 1920s, Toronto Casualty made its biggest mark in automobile insurance. Ernest had loved automobiles ever since his first encounter with "Lizzie" in Saskatchewan. Auto insurance underwent a long experimental period in the 1910s, during which the industry explored the level of risks involved, and various premium and profit structures.

---

10   *Canadian Insurance*, "Merchants and Employers G&A Co. is Refinanced," date unknown.
11   *The Evening Examiner*, "The Ackerman-Dawson Co. Purchase Control of the General Animals Ins. Co.", Peterborough, August 18, 1923.

A 1920 article[12] noted the increased public interest in automobile insurance. "The aggressive campaign carried on by all the companies writing automobile insurance to popularize this form of cover; the growing recognition by the motoring public of its many benefits; the increase in the number of automobiles in the country and the invasion of the motor insurance field by many new companies have all had their effect, and the abstract of automobile insurance written in Canada during the year 1919, shows remarkable increases over the business written in any previous year."

At that time, auto insurance was divided into two types, with fire risk insured separately from other types of loss. Nationally, "Premium income in 1919 was $1,509,957 for automobile insurance inclusive of the fire risk, and $1,902,905 for insurance without the fire risk." The article noted that the industry was still trying to come up with uniform rates that reflected actual experience of losses in the field. "Under the new system of rating, public liability and property damage classes are based upon the list price of the insured car instead of on the horse-power as has been the case in the past."

Automobile technology was still very much in its infancy, with fire risk associated with various makes' wiring and gas tank arrangements. Theft risk, the industry decided, should be based on the make rather than the list price of the car. Make had more to do with the ease of "disposing of" stolen cars.

In 1925, a Toronto Casualty bulletin to its agents boasted that during the year the company had already transacted "the largest automobile insurance business among all companies operating in Canada." The bulletin also noted that the company offered a "uniform and adequate premium... refusing to join in the general scramble for business 'at any old rate'." Toronto Casualty had hit upon a risk and premium structure in which it felt confident.

Toronto Casualty's prominence in the auto insurance field was described by a 1925 article[13] announcing an industry-wide reduction of 20 percent in premium rates. The article listed one hundred companies in Canada selling auto insurance. Net premiums ranked a total of $3,833,905 for the previous year, with Toronto Casualty taking in more than $153,000 of that—more than any other single company.

---

12   *The Financial Post,* "Auto Insurance Grows as Motor Drivers Increase: Uniform Rates and Policies Being Worked Out." Date unknown, 1920.
13   *The Financial Post,* "Auto Insurance Companies Have Recently Reduced Their Rates," April 10, 1925.

Toronto Casualty broke the million-dollar mark for annual cash premium income in 1928. Net claims for the year stood at $492,000, putting the operation in a healthy position according to Ernest.[14]

In 1926, Toronto Casualty broke further new ground in the insurance industry by offering, for the first time in Canada, a comprehensive automobile insurance covering both public liability and property damage to "an unlimited extent."[15] An article in *Saturday Night* magazine featured a photo of Ernest and noted that the move broke several important coverage barriers.

> Recent damage actions have abundantly shown the inadequacy of the ordinary limits in automobile insurance policies and the urgent need of a more comprehensive cover. This new policy goes the whole way and affords the motorist complete protection... $20,000 of liability under it is split three ways by three Canadian companies and the excess above $20,000 is covered by Treaty reinsurance. The new policy also covers the insured driver whilst driving any private car with the owner's consent, and the value of this additional cover will be readily recognized, as it frequently happens that circumstances compel a driver to take the wheel of a friend's car... this policy represents a considerable advance in the extension of automobile insurance cover in Canada. It is creditable that the first company to place such a comprehensive policy on the market should be a purely Canadian company.

The reader should also notice that it was probably the Toronto Casualty Group that shared the liabilities of these ground-breaking auto insurance policies.

---

14 *The Toronto Daily Star*, "Toronto Casualty Income Exceeds Million Dollars," March 6, 1928.

15 *Saturday Night*, "Toronto Casualty Steps in Front with Unlimited Automobile Liability Policy," March 20, 1926.

Toronto Casualty—Too Big, Too Fast?

In 1927, the *Canadian Insurance* magazine[16] examined Toronto Casualty's rapid rise, and in particular, Ernest's impact on the Canadian insurance field. The article suggested that people in the insurance field enjoyed a favourite topic of conversation: *Was Toronto Casualty growing too fast?* And was A.E. Dawson "simply piling up premium income from indifferent business which other companies wouldn't... so that A.E. Dawson would make his fortune and live happy ever after"? The whole insurance community was wondering, said the author, if Toronto Casualty "has reached a financial position which warrants complete confidence."

The article went on to assess the known facts and concluded that Toronto Casualty, and other companies in the group, were indeed sound. (A Canadian dollar at that time was worth roughly thirteen times a present-day dollar.) The article stated:

> The Toronto Casualty made an underwriting profit in 1926 of $30,000. The Canadian General (an associate company) made $5,800. The Merchants and Employers (another associate company) made nearly $30,000. This group is made up of three successful 100 percent Canadian companies with $1,200,000 [nearly $20,112,000 in 2021 dollars] annual premium income.
>
> The Group has pulled through several of the worst years the insurance business has seen and presumably these companies are going to be much stronger in the next few years, which, unless there is another great War, will unquestionably be some of the best business years Canada has ever seen....
>
> It is only reasonable then, to suggest, from the above facts that agents and the public may feel complete confidence in the position and future of this leading group of Canadian companies.

---

16   *Canadian Insurance* "One of the Largest Canadian Insurance Groups Built Up in Five Years is Toronto Casualty, Fire and Marine Insurance Co., and Its Associated Companies,", January 26, 1927.

A Decade of Success

As Ernest was quoted regularly in the *Star*, the *Financial Post*, and the *Globe and Mail*, so too was his wife noted. Together, they appeared in the *Star*'s society pages every month or so. The Dawsons were people to know in Toronto. The mentions were regular and included such brief stories as their travels to New York City, staying at the Biltmore Hotel. In another story, Mr. and Mrs. A.E. Dawson were cited as involved in "a gay event" of the Jarvis Collegiate Institute's Old Girls' and Boys' Association. Lynda was frequently mentioned for her musical activities in the city. The Dawsons were part of Toronto's elite, and their six children were too.

During this period, the family occupied a huge house in Rosedale, on 74 Crescent Road, in Toronto's poshest neighbourhood. A modern mansion now occupies the address, but Rosedale is still posh and impressive. The Dawsons' next-door neighbour was the same multi-millionaire who built Toronto's famous Casa Loma. Ernest would go out to his porch every morning and listen while the millionaire whistled to greet the day for a few minutes. After the brief whistling concert, Ernest would drive in one of his late-model Buicks to work downtown.

The End at Toronto Casualty

Ernest's reign as general manager at the Toronto Casualty Group came to an abrupt end in September 1929. The company had been bought out the previous year by Canadian Insurance Shares, Ltd. A year after the corporate takeover, and roughly a month before Black Friday, the great stock market crash, Canadian Insurance Shares replaced Ernest with *two* men who became the general managers.[17] According to family lore, Ernest had been in Germany, acquiring another company, and returned home to find himself ousted. He resigned.

The *Financial Post* noted the event:

> Active management of the Toronto Casualty, Fire and Marine Insurance company, has been taken over by Canadian Insurance

---

17 *The Financial Post*, "Canadian Insurance Shares Takes Over Active Control," September 12, 1929.

Shares Limited, as of September 2 and W.F. Fess and Paul H. Horst have been appointed general managers as from that date to succeed A.E. Dawson, who has resigned from his connection with the company.

While control of Toronto Casualty was secured by Canadian Insurance Shares as at December 21, 1928, and has been since that time under the general direction of the controlling company, no part had been taken in the active management of the subsidiary. It is understood that the new management will make some changes in policy and that the company will be operated along conservative lines... The Canadian Insurance Shares, Limited, controls Toronto Casualty, Canadian General Insurance, and has incorporated Canadian Re-Insurance Corporation which is at present undergoing development. It is understood that the holding company will also acquire a Western company in the course of a few months, thus completing an all-Canadian group of firms and casualty insurance companies.

Ernest left Toronto Casualty in excellent shape before the stock market crash. He noted in a speech at his last annual meeting,[18]

> With the end of 1928 came the close of what may be considered this company's period of adolescence. It is not, as I conceive it, the function of an insurance company, during its early years, to concern itself primarily or even largely, with the matter of earning profit, but rather to avail itself of every legitimate means of providing for the thorough and widespread and effective establishment of the company, its agency forces and the production of a large volume of business, selected as carefully as circumstances permit.
>
> The past seven years' operations of this company reflect the application of this principle, and it must be admitted with success, since we have today one of the larger incomes from direct agency production in Canada, in fire and casualty insurance business, written

---

18   "Excellent Statement by the Toronto Casualty," [editorial] *Canadian Insurance*, February 22, 1929, page 6.

by a purely Canadian company, the premium income during 1928 being in excess of $1,000,000 from which a profit, not large, but nevertheless a profit, has been derived. Of this income, more than $550,000 has been derived from the company's home Province of Ontario.

After he left the company in 1929, *Canadian Insurance*[19] reviewed Ernest's remarkable performance over the previous decade. The author observed his seemingly golden touch with the many companies he acquired, directed or owned:

> During the eight years in which he [Ernest] has been identified with fire and casualty insurance in Canada... and developing a powerful agency organization through the Dominion. The company has now assets of over $1,250,000 and is transacting a business having a premium income well in excess of $1,000,000 annually. The company is sound and well financed.
>
> In 1924 Mr. Dawson purchased the General Animals Insurance Company, changing its name to Canadian General Insurance Company, and bringing its head office in Toronto. That sound and well-financed company has now assets in excess of $1,000,000 and is transacting annually a very substantial business.
>
> In 1925 he purchased the Merchants & Employers Guarantee & Accident Company, which company is not refinanced, has assets of $700,000, is transacting a substantial volume of business and is throughout the rest of Canada. The company is a Dominion licensed company over twenty years old and is licensed to transact practically all class of fire, automobile, and casualty insurance. It has a paid capital of $200,000 and surplus over and above capital of $120,000....
>
> The operations of this group have had a most significant effect upon the proportion of insurance in Canada transacted by purely

---

19   *Canadian Insurance*, date unknown.

Canadian companies. The total volume of Canadian business very closely [amounts to] $3,000,000 in premiums per annum.

The writer pointed out that when Ernest and the others had founded Toronto Casualty, Canadian firms conducted only 5 percent of the fire and casualty insurance business in Canada. At the time of his resignation, after eight short years, Dawson & Company had doubled the Canadian presence in the industry, "with every prospect of... taking, very rapidly a larger and more important part in the insurance business of this country."

Two months after the Toronto Casualty's new management took place, the company advertised in a large display ad, apparently to reassure customers and to recruit new agents. The *Financial Post* ad[20] read,

> This is an All-Canadian Company equipped to enable its agents to render to their clients a complete Insurance service.
>
> The Company has made a study of the particular requirements of the Canadian insuring public and is in a position to insure against every possible contingency. The representation of this Company will be of decided advantage to every Insurance and Financial Agency, and applications are invited.

The ad ended with bold print, declaring that Canadians could still "Insure With Confidence" with Toronto Casualty.

Before the stock market crash of 1929, Ernest was the darling of the Canadian casualty insurance industry. He appeared frequently in Ontario newspapers, and he and his wife were regular visitors to the society pages. Times changed drastically after that. Ernest does not show up in newspapers until the year 1934, when he suddenly appears in advertisements as a stock securities broker specializing in mines.

---

20   *The Financial Post*, advertisement, November 7, 1929.

CHAPTER 8:
Literary Ambitions

Ernest made a big mark in the insurance world during the late 1910s and 1920s. However, he was, at the same time, pouring his prodigious energies into another ambition: he became a published writer. He wrote and published so much material that I wonder if being a published writer was, in fact, a major ambition, conflicting with his business goals. It is clear that he read and wrote for many hours a week—on top of his varied business activities. I think he wanted to be a writer as much as anything else, but of course he needed to make a living, and insurance was that living. However, under the businessman lurked the man who wanted to be a published writer.

Ernest inherited a love of literature and a profound respect for books, one of the few positive traits that he inherited from his profligate father. The evidence? While in the wilds of Saskatchewan, around 1913, he wrote to his father regarding his upcoming birthday. He did not wish for clothing, a new briefcase, or money. He wanted nothing more than for his father to ship him *books* from the family library. He wanted to read.

He read nearly anything he could get his hands on. Starting with poetry, he read many Victorian writers and copied down lines he enjoyed or admired. In his wooden trunk, I found a dozen little notebooks and calendars. They were not filled with appointments or business matters, but with excerpts from poetry. He read poems from newspapers and magazines and books. He copied love poems, religious poems, and patriotic poems. He copied poems about the beauty of nature—and poems by men and by women. Others he carefully clipped and glued into big notebooks. And when I was a child, decades later, he read me poetry aloud.

One example, from an unknown magazine, was glued into a used bookkeeping notebook, and discussed the "fallen woman." The poem was a typically romantic, probably sexist, handling of its subject.

The Slave Girl

I labored all day in the market,
> Where the feet of the city go by,

But the wage of my toil scarce bought me—
> A place for my head to lie.

So scanty the bread of grim future,
> That the rose of my beauty I sold,

And the wage of the trade secured me
> A lodge in a House of Gold.

O, Master who stood at the forging
> Of the chains of both hunger and ease,

Does my choice of the two displease thee,
> Or have I the best of these!

> *By Inez M. Nichols.*

Another clipping, surrounded by a woodcut illustration of an Aboriginal man in full headdress, went:

INDIAN SUMMER

The rustling leaves with faces turned

Welcome the kiss of the sighing wind,

A melody from a wild bird's throat,

Like the love song of the Indian maid,

Comes from the tangled underbrush

And over all the golden Sunday

Hangs in a haze. The Autumn flowers

Are bathed in a sheen of gold.

The haunting stillness breathes of the souls

Of departed braves.

By John Gruelle

Poetry of the time, by our standards, tended to be wordy, sentimental, saccharin, sexist, racist, emotional, and didactic. It was usually rhymed and rhythmic. People wrote their poems and sent them off to local and national periodicals, which duly printed them. Ernest treasured them all, it seems, and preserved them, and sometimes wrote his own poems along the same lines.

Poetry aside, the early twentieth century was alive with literary energy. Sensitive souls could write poems and essays and books, and actually get them published. One poetry column was entitled "Firelight." One can envision a family reading the column aloud to each other by candlelight or lanterns, the evening's entertainment being the latest poems and stories published in their favourite magazine. Ernest loved to recite and read poetry to his family.

Reviewing Books

In the late 1910s, Ernest became a regular book reviewer for a national magazine, the *Montreal Weekly Witness and Canadian Homestead*. It was an ideal sideline for the insurance man... a chance to read books by Canadian writers and to write and be published every week. In his column, he reviewed two or three books a week from 1918 to 1919. The magazine, as indicated by the title, concerned agriculture as well as news and reviews. The back page of Ernest's literary reviews often concerned raising poultry.

The *Montreal Weekly* had a definite editorial stance on Quebec, which even then posed questions to Canadian identity. The editor, Wilfrid Dougall, wrote to Ernest in April of 1919,

This book was not sent to us for review. So we have purchased it and are sending it to you. It is a book which has given to the French Canadians a great deal of pleasure. It is selling in quantities among them, and they are so enthusiastic over it that its author was suggested as the new leader of the liberal party. With it I am sending you a copy of a book which is not new, but which presents the opposite side of the question. Mr. Seller, the able editor of the "Huntingdon Gleaner", has grown up in the heart of the unavowed struggle that has taken place between the races in the eastern townships, and has seen English localities one after another turning French, partly by natural process, but partly by the intrigue of the church, so that he naturally sees things from a different angle than does Mr. Moor. Very truly, Wilfrid Dougall.

In another letter in July of that year, the editor wrote, "Sending books. I was sorry to hear that you had an attack of the grippe, and very pleased to find that you are again well enough to do reviewing." He said he included a book about the Second Coming, "an extremely controversial subject. And while we must review the book, it is not one to which we desire to give any extended space."

By 1924, Ernest had become the reviewer for *WORLD WIDE*, an eighty-year-old, international magazine, self-described as "a paper with a high mission to Canadians—and help to interpret each to the other, the better motives of the Anglo-Saxon peoples." The masthead urged readers to "Be rational: Think Internationally without being subject to any possible alien propaganda." It also noted that the paper's pages alone "are declared by prominent thinking men and women all over Canada to be 'worth much more than the subscription rate'" (renewed at $2.50 for one year).

For *WORLD WIDE*, Ernest was writing up to five or more reviews a week... a prodigious amount of reading on top of his senior position in the insurance world. He was given a lot of freedom in his reviews, which ranged from two or three paragraphs to several columns. In one letter, dated May 31, 1924, the editor, D. Murray, asked Mr. Dawson to review four books, and more if he could for their special Book Number coming up. Deadline June 10. "Some of the books you will receive will not be worth a great deal of space, but of course, you will use your own judgment in that regard."

Ernest's column enjoyed a regular advertiser: Dodd's Kidney Pills, a famous over-the-counter medication for many decades.

In his wooden trunk, Ernest clipped and scrapbooked the more than 125 literary reviews he published in the two magazines. This side career must have provided him with a great deal of prestige in Canadian literary circles. He was also a member of the Toronto Arts and Letters Society. I have no way of knowing how widely read his two magazines were, but WORLD WIDE was eighty years old and must have had some cachet.

Ernest's personal views on matters crept into his reviews. One, regarding *My Fight for Irish Freedom*, by Dan Breen (Dec. 20, 1924, WORLD WIDE), included the comments:

> There is little attempt in this volume to establish by argument, any claim to national [Irish] independence. The thing is sought by violent means—and without any thought of reason or right or other consideration. The many whose mistaken belief is that the Irish are a nation rather than a collection of tribes have some claim to sympathy in their efforts towards achievement and for their many mistakes in their attempts to force upon Ireland unwanted political and economic considerations. The land has long since paid the price. Breen advances nothing of this. He only knew he wanted to fight and he certainly achieved his desire. I am not at all sure that he was a "splendid Rebel."

In other columns, Ernest considered problems that could very well have been written today. He reviewed *The Narcotic Drug Problem* by Ernest S. Bishop.

> This book is a result of a wide and varied experience of narcotic drug addiction, and many years spent in the attempted solution of its problems. It appears to be an honest and sympathetic attempt to secure the welfare of society as related to this addiction and to present the force of a conclusion resulting from a wide experience that drug addiction is a disease, and should be treated as such. The author hopes that a more comprehensive knowledge of the subject will result in individuals suffering from a disease of this nature being treated as sick persons and returned to health

instead of being "turned back upon their own resources after inadequate treatment."

Other Publications

During the 1910s and 1920s, Ernest also wrote for various insurance journals and papers. He gave a speech in Toronto, describing "My Ideal Insurance Agent," and the text was reprinted in two periodicals, including the *Financial Post*. The *Post* often printed essays on the insurance industry, but they were usually by the federal Superintendent of Insurance.

Ernest also wrote essays and op-ed letters to the editor. One article concerned the training of the English sheepdog—probably from his personal experience in Derbyshire. Another appeared in the *Spectator* and described an Ontario man named Silas who had legendary strength and an astounding work ethic (a story he repeated in his later novel).

Ernest was less successful in selling his fiction, however. He submitted a story called "The Roan" to various publishers with no success. The story concerned an arduous adventure as a cattle drover, with a lost roan cow. The story was undoubtedly drawn from his experiences in Derbyshire.

In his late fifties, he wrote a long, 355-page, romantic novel, *In the Shadow of Orkis*, which was rejected by Macmillan in February 1961. The editor, Jack Gray, after explaining that the novel lacked "tension and reality at many points," added a personal note, hoping that that just writing the book had given Ernest "great pleasure and satisfaction."

Business was simply too small a field for Ernest's wide-ranging intellect. He turned to writing and to book-reviewing to consider the whole range of human experience and history. As a writer, he gave himself permission to consider emotion and love, and to allow his imagination to bloom fully. During his years in prison and in retirement, he continued to write, and penned hundreds of pages of essays, poems, and stories. Writing was the activity that continued, consistently, throughout his life.

As Ernest's granddaughter, I have inherited this need to write. And sometimes, reading the latest rejection notice in my email, I sympathize with this man profoundly. But, like Grandad, rejections from publishers never stop me from writing.

A Happy Day in Rosedale

The 1920s were probably the happiest period of Ernest's life. In the community, he was a successful and respected business executive, living in Toronto's most prestigious neighbourhood, with his wife and six children. Life in Rosedale had come as far from his rough, abused childhood as he could possibly imagine. Life was good.

Lynda was by then an accomplished pianist, singer (soprano), and choir leader. Years later, Ernest describes just one day in Rosedale, in that good life—getting up early on a school day to the sound of music as his children took turns fighting for the bathroom and, alternately, the piano. He describes the day's early moments at the piano, the focal point of Dawson family life.

The story, called "Octave," is from a manuscript in Grandad's wooden trunk. My cousin Ken Howard says that he had seen it published somewhere in a large format magazine, but I've never seen it.

The story describes, in its poignant details, Ernest's love for Lynda. He clearly adored her, and felt great pride in her achievements.

> Harry [the eldest boy], without so much as pausing on the landing continued on down to the living room, pulling on his dressing gown the while.

> …from the living room came a new series of sounds as Harry groped among the piano keys for an inspiration. Presently it came in the form of "One Fine Day" which he sang at the top of his voice, accompanying himself at the piano. This and other selections occupied him until he knew that one of his brothers was using the bathroom, when he went upstairs again and bullied the younger boy into letting him in to share it.

After a tumultuous breakfast and preparations for school, Ernest walked outside to his car, to go to the office.

> As I came level with the sidewalk at the front of the house I heard the piano again and my wife's voice lifting into song once more, and I knew beyond peradventure that during her morning's housekeeping duties she would go twenty times to the piano to

express herself in song and music, playing and singing something that came to her mind, or perfecting some thing or other with which she was not quite as yet satisfied...

Sometime during the morning at my office, my secretary came in and said "Mrs. Dawson is on the 'phone—shall I have her put through now?"...

"Hallo, Dad," came my wife's voice. "Sorry to disturb you. What do you think? Sir Ernest MacMillan [Toronto Symphony conductor and Mendelssohn Choir director] phoned me just now. He wants us to sing at the Symphony Concert. Isn't that fine?"...

"Yes, that's grand. Is your choir up to it?"

"No, not at the moment, of course. I can have them up to it in plenty of time, however."

For some years my wife had taken in hand a score or so of the neighbours' daughters, ranging in age from about eight to twelve years of age, and had trained them into a choir of more than passing note. They sang—and looked—like angels... This invitation to her choir to sing at this outstanding event was somewhat in the nature of a "command" performance and placed the seal of authority and authenticity as it were, upon my wife's efforts.

Into this labour of love she had put all her energies and her considerable talent. Her association with these children kept her young. She had the freshness, the vigour, and the youthfulness of outlook of a girl when thus engaged...

This choir created an additional routine of musical activity about the house. A further load upon the long-suffering piano—practices, rehearsals, auditions—were apt to be in progress at any time after school and I would frequently find myself crowded out of my comfortable corner into another room, or out onto the lawn. To this would be added the ceaseless playing and singing of any or all of the members of the family when they came in. It seemed that the piano was always in use. I cannot quite decide if my ability to tolerate and even enjoy all this musical confusion arises from some unsuspected depths of appreciation or enjoyment of music, or if it merely arose from personal pride and delight in the happy throng which all but continuously milled in and about the house…

This had been created and inspired by my wife, who seemed to have experienced in life no frustration other than an inability to discover more than twenty-four hours a day in which to crowd her musical activities, run her house, and raise her children.

Music was in and on the air in the house before the radio filled the air waves of the world with song. Penetrating to every room were showers of music—sprinklings and downpours of song. There would be calm and storm, cloudbursts and hurricanes, sweeping through hallways and stairways. Piano or piano and voice—the tide would now ebb, now flow.

On the evening of the exciting invitation to be part of the symphony choir, Ernest found Lynda already planning the girls' outfits and debating the music the girls would sing. The debate became the central topic at supper. News of the invitation had spread through the community, and after supper more than twenty visitors dropped in to congratulate and argue about the musical choices. One visitor broke into the debate with fifteen minutes of boogie-woogie on the piano, to a "pandemonium of laughter and loud singing."

Finally, at the end of the day, Ernest climbed the stairs to bed.

My wife turned out the lights and seated herself at the piano. For a little while I heard her playing and singing softly. Then she came slowly, contentedly up the stair. She was humming softly—humming—humming!

This day surely defined happiness for Ernest—one of the clearest memories that he carried with him into darker times.

CHAPTER 9:
The Cataclysm–1929

*I*n late 1929, Ernest's high-flying world came crashing down on two fronts. As previously discussed, he was forced to resign in a corporate takeover. Secondly, he probably lost much of his fortune in the stock market crash of that year.

In piecing together what happened to Ernest, I must depend on disparate newspaper clippings, his actual resignation letter, and indirect evidence of his activities from Lakefield school records.

Until October 29, investors were confident that their stocks would keep climbing in value. Many people, probably including Ernest, bought stocks "on the margin." This meant they took out loans from banks to cover stock purchases, counting on increased stock values to pay back the loans at a later date. One writer says, "a 10 percent margin payment would permit them to buy 10 times as much market gain as if they had bought the stock outright."[21] Like a stack of cards, the whole financial fiction came crashing down on October 29. And banks began to call in their loans. Many stock owners lost the stocks they had put up in collateral, now greatly devalued, and were stuck with huge loans to pay off.

Fortunately for insurance companies, stocks were purchased with outright cash payments. So when the banks began calling in their loans after the market crash, insurance companies were immune from these margin calls. "No holder of a life, fire, or casualty policy in Canada has during the year

---

21   Jeffers, Wellington, *The Globe and Mail,* "How Toronto Speculators Tried to Halt the Financial Disaster of 25 Years Ago," October 30, 1954, page 19.

lost any of the protection afforded by his policy through the inability of any company to honour its obligations," wrote G.D. Finlayson, Superintendent of Insurance in Ottawa.[22] Just four months after the crash, fire and casualty insurance was still doing well in Canada, with more than $57 million in fire premiums and $38 million in casualty net premiums.[23]

Individual stock investors—probably including Ernest—were not immune from margin calls, however, and many lost their paper fortunes because their stocks were now valued at a fraction of their purchase value—often less than the loan amounts. Selling the stock could not repay the loans. (This situation resembles the housing market crash of 2008, when homeowners found that their mortgaged houses were now worth less than the mortgages they owed.)

Undoubtedly, Ernest's personal investments and the Toronto Casualty group's assets plummeted to the depths in value. The *Toronto Daily Star*'s index of sixteen key Canadian stocks lost $300 million on Black Thursday, falling about a million dollars per minute.[24]

Ernest may well have been in financial trouble earlier than that, however. In 1928, all four of his sons had to be withdrawn from The Grove (Lakefield School).[25] This began the period described by my father, Don, as tumultuous and stressful. "We were millionaires one day, and paupers the next," he recalled to me. "One day we would be attending Lakefield, and the next day we'd be in Jarvis Collegiate public school." He said that much of his childhood involved these wild swings in the family fortunes. Suddenly, there would be no more triumphal rides to Lakefield in the yearly new Buick. Instead, the boys would find themselves at the ignominious registration at Jarvis Collegiate—in last year's Buick.

---

22 Finlayson, G.D., *The Globe and Mail*, "Canadian Insurance Survives Depression Without a Casualty," January 3, 1934, page 19.
23 *The Globe and Mail*, "Amazing Growth is Shown in Insurance Since 1880," February 19, 1930, page 14.
24 *The Globe and Mail*, "After the fall," October 29, 1979, page F32.
25 Young, Kelly, Communications and Constituent Relations Assistant, Lakefield College School, personal communications, 2017. School records show that all four brothers were withdrawn in 1928, Ken was pulled in 1929, but Don graduated in 1934. This confusing record simply confirms Don's recollection of extreme instability.

My father vowed never to subject his family to such a roller coaster ride.[26] He studied a trade that would provide steady employment—land surveying—and moved as far west as he could to get away from the volatility of Toronto finances, and perhaps, his father's eventual corruption. His sister Darrell also moved west, and married a staid civil servant, Don's best friend Phil Howard. She lost, through her father's swings of fortune, her private school education and the chance to go to university.

For Lynda, it must have been a dreadful period. It must have been hard to maintain the family's high social standing while Ernest's job loss and huge financial losses threatened everything—their home in Rosedale, the annual new Buick, and the children's education. One can imagine her consternation as Ernest tried to explain his margin investments—maybe in 1928—the sudden drop in value of his stocks and bonds in 1929—his sudden jobless status—and their lack of cash for household expenses. For Lynda, it had to be a series of bitter pills to swallow. As adults, their children later reported loud arguments between Ernest and Lynda. Theirs was a house in frequent turmoil and despair.

In the late 1920s, however, the Toronto Casualty Group of companies was in great shape. All three of the main companies were reporting increased earnings. Despite the fact that the group had been bought out by Canadian Insurance Shares, Limited, the new owners had not interfered with actual management of Toronto Casualty and the others. In the fall or late summer of 1929, Ernest confidently left for Germany to do business. His mission in Germany was typical of the big corporate deals he seemed to carry off with aplomb. It was probably the matter of the Assurance Union of Hamburg, Germany.[27] There he reinsured that company's Canadian accounts with his own company, Merchants & Employers Guarantee & Accident Company. In so doing, he brought in $50,000 in premiums ($838,000 in 2021 dollars). It was a nice deal.

Merchants & Employers Guarantee was involved in the heady world of the reinsurance business. Thus, the primary insurance company (Assurance

---

26   Hellum, Kare, personal communication. Don Dawson confided this vow to his friend, Kare Hellum. Kare remembers Don's sadness and bitterness about his childhood, and the reason for his choice as a salaryman with a steady, if modest, income.
27   *Canadian Insurance*, "Merchants and Employers G& A is Refinanced," date unknown, 1929.

Union) was reinsured by Merchants & Employers Guarantee against catastrophic losses above and beyond the reserves of the primary company. For instance, in the case of a hurricane or a flood, the primary company might pay out a million dollars in claims, while the reinsurer paid an agreed amount—say three or four million—for claims above that level. Reinsurance is a way of spreading the relatively low risk, but higher liability, of catastrophic events among several players, with the primary insurer paying a premium to the reinsurer (in this case, $50,000).

Family lore has it that when Ernest returned from his trip to Germany, he discovered that he had been deposed from his position of general manager of Toronto Casualty. It was a palace coup of sorts.

We have two different dates for Ernest's resignation. The first comes from a September 1929 article about his ouster as general manager.[28] According to the article, Ernest resigned his connections with Toronto Casualty at that time. The second date is his actual resignation letter (from the wooden trunk), which was dated November 19, 1929, a couple of weeks after the stock market crash. His letter to President Mr. G. Larrett Smith did not cite the reason for his resignation. I think this resignation was the result of the new owners taking control, and possibly his role as general manager of some of the other companies in the Toronto Casualty Group.

Ernest's resignation was probably an ugly affair. He announced his intention to stay with the Merchants & Employers Guarantee & Accident Company, the reinsurance company. When he left Toronto Casualty, however, he spirited away the senior members of the Toronto Casualty staff, most of whom had been associated with him in his fire and casualty activities "from inception." Such wholesale raiding of personnel is part of the reason companies now insist on a non-compete clause in hiring contracts. Such clauses prevent working in competing companies for a year or so after leaving a company. However, such clauses clearly were not in effect at that time, and Ernest took his whole crew with him. Ernest also remained chief agent for Employers Reinsurance Corporation, at the time the largest casualty reinsurance company in America. This company had many important contracts in

---

28   *The Financial Post,* "Canadian Insurance Shares Takes Over Active Control," September 12, 1929.

Canada. We do not know how long Ernest stayed with this company, or Merchants & Employers Guarantee & Accident.

It is not surprising that after Ernest robbed the company of its senior executives, Toronto Casualty advertised that "applications are invited" to represent the company[29] along with assurances that people could "insure with confidence" in Toronto Casualty.

One might ask, why was Canadian Insurance Shares so anxious to sever ties with Ernest? He had served the company well for nearly a decade. One clue is in the company announcement that the new management would henceforth conduct company business along "conservative" lines. Does this mean that Ernest was seen as too much of a risk taker? Or was he doing something illegal or unethical in his management of investments for the company? He had opened his own brokerage firm in 1925—was this firm involved, a conflict of interest? We have no evidence of any illegal or unethical behaviour here, just that his personal finances were probably in disarray at the time.

In addition to the corporate losses in assets due to the market crash, Ernest no doubt lost the good part of his personal fortune to margin calls. His sudden change in status, both financially and in reputation, probably terrified his family.

During the next four years, as the Great Depression set in, Ernest effectively disappeared from the media. He is not mentioned once in the *Globe*, the *Star*, or any of the other Toronto papers. He is no longer quoted as a director, a corporate officer, or as an expert on casualty insurance. Nothing in the wooden trunk illuminates this period.

Ernest was probably scrambling desperately for a new foothold in the business world. He must have lost his positions in the various Toronto Casualty Group companies. I have been unable to find any solid evidence of what actually happened. It was, however, probably a series of unfortunate events.

He finally reappears in the newspapers in 1934, advertising his services with A.E. Dawson & Company as a humble securities broker, specializing in mining stocks. He started all over again, selling stocks despite another market crash on July 21, 1934. And he was doing business with the most speculative of all securities—gold mining and oil and gas stocks.

---

29   *The Financial Post*, block advertisement, November 7, 1929.

Ernest probably did not have much money to work with, but he may have still had his reputation as a respected insurance man. He still may have had a good name on Bay Street.

The family was now riding on Ernest's more dangerous financial roller coaster, at risk of even greater swings in fortune. There were no more new Buicks in the fall.

The Dawson Legacy in Canadian Casualty Insurance

For all his later faults and sins, Ernest Dawson bequeathed Canada with a nearly hundred-year-old legacy in industry. He was an aggressive, ambitious creator and administrator. He helped create a group of Canadian-based companies that have played a prominent role in the country's casualty insurance industry for a hundred years.

It's interesting to follow the bloodlines of the three major companies he helped found or acquire:
- Toronto Casualty and Marine Insurance Company,
- The General Animals Insurance Company, and the
- Merchants' and Employers' Guarantee & Accident Company.

Two of these companies have survived into the present day as major Canadian insurance companies, albeit with new names and corporate identities. The third survived until 1989.

Insurance companies have complex, extended histories. In fact, these histories can be illustrated with corporate genealogy charts, similar to the family genealogy charts. These corporate charts show mergers, acquisitions, renaming, and reorganizations over the decades. Ernest Dawson's companies, established or acquired in the 1920s, are no exception. Their descendants have survived decades, in fact almost a century now, eventually becoming part of global megalith insurance companies, General Insurance of Britain, and Aviva Insurance of Canada.

Fortunately, for me, insurance companies themselves keep track of these corporate family histories. Margie Watts of the Aviva Insurance Company provided the complex histories, shown here, of Ernest's major companies. We are grateful for her research.

Toronto Casualty

Ernest was one of twelve stockholders who established Toronto Casualty and Marine Insurance Company as an Ontario casualty insurance company on July 21, 1921. The other stockholders were Alfred John Walker Greig, Albert Edward Wilson, Reuben May Sliter, Richard Haliburton Greer, Goldwin Larrett Smith, Forbes Godfrey, Charles Haydn Ackerman, Thomas Metcalf Murdoch, Valentine Frederick Stock, Laurel Cole Palmer, and Wallace Arthur Scott. Together these men bankrolled Toronto Casualty. They provided the capital assets needed to back up any insurance company's assurance that it could pay claims as necessary.

A year later, the company changed its name to Toronto Casualty Fire and Marine Insurance Company and in 1930 to Toronto General Insurance Company. In 1937 it transferred its assets and became a federally chartered company with the same name (beginning as a provincially chartered firm in Ontario).

During the 1920s, Ernest Dawson was the vice president and general manager of Toronto Casualty. He was the most-quoted figure for the firm and its associated companies for most of the decade. Just before the stock market crash of 1929, when Ernest left the company, all three members of the Toronto Casualty Group were in healthy financial shape, and were among the most prominent Canadian firms in the casualty insurance business.

Canadian General Insurance

Ernest Dawson did not originate the General Animals Insurance Company of Canada, but under his management, Toronto Casualty acquired the firm in 1924, changing its name to the Canadian General Insurance Company. In so doing, Dawson also moved the firm from its livestock-insuring niche market to a more general casualty insurance firm.

The two firms, Toronto and Canadian General Insurance companies, did business for another sixty years, often advertising casualty insurance together in the same advertisement. They amalgamated with each other on January 1,

1994, and were then known as the Canadian General Insurance Company. In 1997, a cash buyout of Can$600 million took place.[30] In 1998, the Canadian General Insurance group amalgamated with the General Accident Assurance Company of Canada. They became the CGU Insurance Company of Canada in 1999. A year later, CGU amalgamated with Commercial Union Assurance Company of Canada and continued as CGU Insurance Company. On December 31, 1999, CGU amalgamated with CAN General Insurance Company. The new firm became known as Aviva Canada in 2003.

Today, Aviva is now one of Canada's largest casualty and property insurers.

Merchants' and Employers' Guarantee & Accident Company

Ernest Dawson stayed with the Merchants' and Employers' Guarantee & Accident Company briefly for a few years after he left the Toronto Casualty Group. The company originated in 1913 under a federal licence. In 1924 Ernest Dawson and others purchased the company[31] for the Toronto Casualty Group, bringing with it a million dollars in premium income.

In its new corporate home, the company did well, according to the *Globe and Mail*.[32] One article stated, "The Merchants and Employers' Insurance Company is one of three important all-Canadian companies operating under what is known as the Toronto Casualty Insurance Company group, which is rapidly developing along successful and national lines under the general management of A.E. Dawson of Toronto."

By 1931 Ernest had disappeared from Merchants' roster—he no longer served on its board of directors or upper management. However, the company survived, becoming the Consolidated Fire & Casualty Company in 1931. At that time, the company announced new management and owned capital of $2 million. 1976 was the last mention of Consolidated's operations we have been able to find in newspapers. Officially, the company went into inactive

---

30 Young, Peter, *A Premium Business, A History of General Accident,* Granta Editions, 1999, page 235.
31 *The Ottawa Journal*, "Further Consolidation Canadian Fire Insurance Organization," October 12, 1925, page 14.
32 *Toronto Globe and Mail,* "Merchants & Employers Insurance Co. Expands," February 10, 1927, page 12.

status in September 1987. The company had survived fifty-eight years after the crash.

*　*　*

Ernest Dawson launched or acquired three healthy casualty insurance corporations in the 1920s. He was associated with them only during the twenties, but he got them started as healthy Canadian corporations that survived the Great Depression and went on to do business for decades after that. Two of the businesses merged and recreated themselves, with assets surviving in today's Aviva Insurance Company. Aviva Canada in 2016 boasts premiums of Can$4,405 million, and the recent acquisition of RBC (Royal Bank of Canada) insurance.

The story comes full circle with this simple fact: Ernest's grandson, Timothy Dawson of Toronto, is an Aviva policyholder. He didn't realize it, but he's keeping his business in the family.

CHAPTER 10:
The Securities Game in the 1930s

Only two geological maps in Ernest's wooden trunk provide any clues as to his activities during the 1930s and '40s. To find out what happened to him during those years, I turned to newspaper records. These were sparse too. He was no longer the go-to man for the press on casualty insurance. All that I could find were his advertisements as a securities dealer. His display ads in the Toronto newspapers began in 1934, when a brief boom in mining stocks took place. The ads continued until the late '30s.

From 1930 to 1934, Ernest appears to have been booted out from all his corporate positions in the Toronto Casualty Group. The evidence? His singular absence from the newspapers with regards to any of these companies. During the 1920s he was an officer or part owner of several of the Toronto Casualty Group companies. His name came up regularly. But during the thirties, nothing. It is possible that he made some money being bought out, as part of financial settlements for withdrawing from the various firms. He must have had some savings, however, because his family continued living in Rosedale.

It was a terrible time to go *into* the securities business, especially as a broker of mining stocks. Christopher Armstrong, the Canadian historian of the securities business during those years, says, in *Blue Skies and Boiler Rooms: Buying and Selling Securities in Canada, 1870-1940*:

Thus the brokerage business was in dire straits during the depression, particularly after Britain left the gold standard in September 1931. The low point came in mid-1932, when the indices of share prices even fell below levels reached in the post-war recession of 1921. Trading volume on the stock exchange also plummeted to pitiful lows compared to the pre-crash period. Though a boom in mining stocks helped bring slightly better times in 1933 and 1934, recovery proved painfully slow. No wonder many brokers were forced to give up the game, squeezed inexorably by their creditors' demands and the stubborn slowness of the economy to emerge from the depths of depression.

With brokers going out of business in droves, and the public trust in their profession at an all-time low, Ernest actually entered the fray. Between August 1929 and November 1932, Armstrong reports that nineteen brokerages in the Toronto Stock Exchange went out of business, while only seven new firms were established.

Banks had hardened from the easy credit days of the previous decade, although many went easy on all but the most egregious of their clients, including many brokers up to their necks in margin debt. Then, in 1930, Britain withdrew from the gold standard, thus striking a huge blow on mining stocks. There was a slight reprieve in 1933 and 1934, when the United States raised the price of gold from $20 per ounce to $35. Mining stocks recovered slightly.

I found Ernest's first advertisements, from 1934, as a mining stocks broker. It is still hard to know why he went into this business, when it seemed so desperately low. It may have been that it was the only avenue open to him, after falling out from the insurance industry. Ernest's sheer hubris might also have brought him into the brokerage business—his hope and confidence in himself, his positive temperament (perhaps arrogance?)—a perspective that had served him well through the past two decades. Family legend says that he lost millions at various times, but he rebuilt his fortunes several times again.

Whatever his motives, Ernest moved into a new office for himself as a securities broker. His address? The elegant Federal Building, at the corner of Queen and Dalhousie in Toronto. The building, known for its imposing clock tower, also featured two lions rampant at the entrance. Ernest established a stylish, dignified location for his new business. No doubt his clients were impressed.

Mining securities has never been a field for the faint of heart. In that way, Ernest was perfect for his new role. He was a gambler at heart, as evinced by his love for high-stakes card games to his betting on the Great Wheelbarrow Race. He also engaged in real-estate speculation in the early 1910s. He played bridge for stakes nearly every week. The stock market offered a way to indulge in real-world gambles, leaning on his reputation as a respectable insurance executive to persuade his clients to join the gamble. And after twenty-five years, Ernest was a salesman again, but now instead of insurance he was selling highly speculative securities. And now, his entire business was centred on one central gamble—the success of prospective gold mines.

Advertising for Gold Stocks

During the 1930s, A.E. Dawson & Company advertised a series of gold-mining securities in the *Globe and Mail,* the *Toronto Daily Star,* and the *Financial Post.* Although the company no doubt sold other mining and resource stocks, it did not advertise other base metal mines, diamonds, or oil. Only gold. Ernest apparently loved the whole idea of gold. Like no other commodity, then as now, gold promised riches and glamour to investors.

I wanted to know what happened to Ernest after he left the insurance game so abruptly in 1929. Was he on the up-and-up, raising money for legitimate mining operations? Or was he a crook from the beginning, promoting sketchy operations? Or, given the times and the Bay Street environment, a little of both? He seems to have been active in securities from at least 1926, when he established his company on the Toronto Board of Trade.[33]

To find out what happened, I surveyed published material on the mining stock and companies he advertised through A.E. Dawson & Company. This evidence in the public domain gives spotty clues as to Ernest's activities, if not a direct account. It is impossible to evaluate the truth of many of the published mining development reports—for the most part, however, I accepted the published accounts at face value. The list of mining concerns leaves us

---

33   *The Globe and Mail,* display ad, April 26, 1937.

with doubts about Ernest's ability to identify successful operations, and about his legitimate securities activities.

My examination of mining-stocks advertisements during the thirties shows that Ernest was just one of dozens of Toronto brokers doing the same thing. The newspapers were full of ads and columns offering insider's tips on the mining industry. All the brokers advertised various mining operations, and they all cloaked their sales pitches in optimistic but conservative language. Despite the losses of the stock market crash, there were still enough Canadians to finance many brokers' endeavours.

The Stocks Ernest Sold from 1934 to 1940

First, Ernest did sell stocks to capitalize mainstream, legitimate mining operations. These included:
- Malartic Mines,
- Hudson Patricia Gold Mines Ltd.,
- Doreva Gold Mines,
- Doreva-related oil wells, and
- Big Master Consolidated Mines.

Malartic was a real gold-producing area that is still mined today.[34] Hudson Patricia mines were in northwestern Ontario and included eight producing mines. Ernest probably also sold stock to capitalize Doreva Gold Mines, in Quebec, but after some development they disappeared from market reports after 1939. Doreva shifted to oil exploration, which Ernest was heavily involved with in California. Unfortunately, these wells did not appear to produce oil. Big Master was a major promotion for Ernest, with many large display ads. Like Doreva mines, they just disappeared from the record.

Secondly, Ernest promoted what was probably a completely depleted mine, the Ruby Queen Silver Mines in Idaho. This mine, if it was real, lay in a completely mined-out area that had not been truly productive for decades. Ernest was listed as on the board of directors for this mine.

Thirdly, Ernest was involved with two mining operations clearly linked to stock fraud. These were the Wylie-Dominion Gold Mines and the

---

34 *The Globe and Mail*, McGee, Niall, "Canada's junior miners hammered by a string of technical blunders," July 13, page 87.

Chappie-Mammoth Gold Mines. Ernest was a director of the Wylie-Dominion mines, but they were prevented from selling their properties by a lawsuit brought by irate prospectors and shareholders. Apparently, money from a stock offering was collected but not invested in the mining operation. Also, the directors—including Ernest, we presume—were not lawfully chosen, said the suit.

Chappie-Mammoth was named as a co-defendant in the U.S. indictments by the Securities and Exchange Commission. The stock was apparently worthless and simply used as a shell company for defrauding victims.

A Typical Bay Street Operator

For the most part, this brief survey tells us that Ernest was probably typical of the slick Toronto mining securities operators during the mid-to-late 1930s. He promoted and sold shares of some real gold concerns, but most of them never panned out into real production. Many were mined-out properties or lying on the fringes of real producing areas. He did not appear to have lucked out with new discoveries of substantial mines. He sold stocks for ore bodies that were unproductive, depleted, or outright fraudulent.

Both the Wylie-Dominion and Chappie-Mammoth associations indicate that Ernest was comfortable working on the wrong side of honest or ethical practice. In that regard, he was probably typical of mining securities brokers at the time.

Author Christopher Armstrong describes scores of stock frauds during this era, with only the big scams getting much attention.[35] Armstrong noted the brief boom in mining stocks in Canada in 1933–1934, when Ernest's advertising began. The boom appeared in response to the raising of U.S. gold to $35 per ounce.

The boom, he said, resulted in the appearance of "high pressure pitches to prospective customers across North America ... In searches of bigger gains, individuals can display an astonishing combination of cupidity and naivety. Governments had a hard time protecting them from their own stupidity, yet felt some obligation to counter outright dishonesty."

---

35 Armstrong, Christopher, *Blue Skies and Boiler Rooms; Buying and Selling Securities in Canada 1870-1940,* University of Toronto Press, Toronto, 1997, page 7.

Ernest advertised and sold, for the most part, worthless stocks. Nonetheless, he and his clients made money on the ups and downs of stock values in the market. Ernest had to be a hustler, albeit a gentleman hustler. He was part of the reason Canada earned its bad name for mining stock swindles. He was part of what the U.S. Securities Exchange Commission (SEC) called The Canadian Problem.

Ernest seems to have suffered bad judgment. The most generous interpretation I can offer is that he fell for bad prospects. Not being a geologist, was he, in turn, deceived by prospectors and mining engineers? He may have been. Maybe the spectacular ore findings were falsified. Or maybe his "hot" mines just petered out when the digging began and when speculators had sucked the stock dry. The California oil wells he promoted never struck oil.

Ernest also appeared to keep bad company. The Wylie-Dominion mines should have been a warning to his clients. Proceeds of stock sales were allegedly never turned over to actual company operations. Where did all that money go? It would be worth three million in today's dollars. If the stock was "unlawfully issued," and he was on the board, the operation looks like it was an out-and-out cash-grab scam. All this took place early in his career as a securities dealer and may have set the groundwork for later illegal acts. It was at least bad company, since he could not have acted alone in the scheme.

Eventually, Ernest seems to have tired of the high risks of mining securities and moved into the more reliable field of outright stock fraud. This period began in the late 1930s. While gold mines were fraught with uncertainty and risk, the gullibility and greed of stock investors could be counted on as much more reliable, predictable resources.

Swindler

Dawson Mining Stock Activities During the 1930s

The 1930s were the period during which Ernest Dawson made the transition from the insurance industry to being an independent securities dealer. To assess his practice during this period—his success, the legitimacy of the stock, and his honesty—I examined the history of the stocks he advertised in the newspapers. The details of these stocks, and the mines they referred to, are discussed below.

They show Ernest as selling a mixture of real, depleted, and fraudulent mines.

Legitimate Mines—Some Successful, Others Not

Malartic Mines

Ernest advertised with a free map and information[36] about the Malartic gold-mining areas in October 1941. These proven Quebec gold fields were discovered in the late 1920s[37] with several exploratory mines established by 1940. One of the mines, East Malartic Mines, produced an average recovery of just over $5 per ton in 1942. Another, Malartic Gold Fields, Ltd., turned a new profit per share of 10.3 cents in 1948, long after Ernest served time and was released from prison.[38]

Various Malartic mines appeared to be legitimate operations, probably with legitimate shares offered through A.E. Dawson & Company. The area is still mined—Malartic is currently Canada's largest gold mine. Malartic stocks appear to be one of Ernest's legitimate offerings.

---

36 *The Globe and Mail,* display ad, October 7, 1941, page 16.
37 *The Globe and Mail,* "Discoveries are Made at Quebec Malartic," July 24, 1928, page 3.
38 *The Globe and Mail,* "Malartic Gold Around Corner," April 14, 1949, page 24.

Hudson Patricia Gold Mines Ltd.

In May of 1936, A.E. Dawson & Company pronounced, in a modest display ad,[39] that the Hudson Patricia Gold Mines Limited were "underpriced at present market. Mill goes into operation in a few days time, putting Hudson Pat. on an earning basis." Found in iron formations, these mines were discovered in a remote northwestern Ontario wilderness area. At first, all men and supplies had to be flown in[40] [41] with establishment of power and roads to come later. By January 1936, five mines were producing, with eight producing by October of the same year.

As with most mining operations, the Hudson Patricia mine required a great deal of outside financing for development. The mines found support in a New York banking house[42] for venture capital.

From newspaper reports on the area, this A.E. Dawson stock offering appears to have been a legitimate gold-mining prospect, although we know nothing of its earnings.

Doreva Gold Mines and California Oil

A.E. Dawson and Co. heavily promoted the promising Doreva Gold Mines between 1936 and 1938.[43] [44] [45] The property in question lay in the Bousquet-Cadillac ore zone. Doreva held the "largest contiguous group" of claims along the zone, according to the *Globe*.[46] The large A.E. Dawson display ads were printed, complete with maps of the ore area, and the claimed that "In Every Portfolio of Mining Securities There Should Be Some Shares of Doreva Gold Mines Limited." The shares were "bought, sold, and quoted" by A.E. Dawson & Company—as well as many other securities dealers. The *Globe* covered explorations by Doreva extensively, noting that two main veins

---

39   *The Globe and Mail,* display ad, May 1936, page 14.
40   *The Globe and Mail,* "Northern Air Travel Links Mining Regions," October 10, 1927, page 6.
41   *The Globe and Mail,* "High Find Reported at Rainbow Lake," July 27, 1927, page 6.
42   *The Globe and Mail,* Hudson Patricia Gold Ltd Drifting on 325-Foot Levels," March 7, 1935, page 16.
43   *The Globe and Mail,* "Doreva Takes on Oil Properties," July 8, 1938, page 21.
44   *The Globe and Mail,* display ad, December 4, 1936, page 27.
45   *The Globe and Mail,* display ad, January 27, 1937, page 23.
46   *The Globe and Mail,* "Sagamore Property Acquired by Doreva," December 3, 1936, page 25.

had been found[47] during drilling, with occurrence of visible gold below the original discovery. Work continued, assuming that these reports were truthful accounts.

Doreva struggled to continue drilling and assaying. Roads and electricity reached the property, but exploration work shut down in the spring of 1937, due to lack of financing. Operations resumed[48] after 1.5 million shares were issued and in 1939, and a series of transactions allowed further work to continue.[49] Ernest probably sold these stocks.

Doreva stocks appeared in the *Globe* until June 1939, after which the mine no longer appeared in the listings.

Doreva was apparently a legitimate Dawson mining gamble that did not pan out in the long haul. How much money Ernest made or lost on the company is unknown. However, Doreva diversified, investing in oil leases in San Luis Obispo County, California, and in Texas.[50] A.E. Dawson & Company announced the shift to oil properties in the *Globe*.

Ernest himself subsequently appeared in California to supervise drilling of two oil wells, according to his letters. In the letters, however, he was working on wells in Palos Verdes, near west Los Angeles, which is two hundred miles from San Luis Obispo. I could not find the relationship between the two drilling areas.

How Ernest got associated with the oil wells is unknown, but he describes the drilling operations in detail[51] to his wife. The wells were real oil explorations. Somehow the two wells were linked to oil operations in Canada, he said. He was optimistic in his letters to Lynda. "It puts into the future a most valuable royalty income for us if and when we discover oil in commercial quantity in Canada."

The fact that neither operation in California struck oil was another case of a Dawson gamble—a very expensive one—that did not pan out, according to subsequent letters. As he told Lynda, "It takes oil to make an oil well."

---

47 *The Globe and Mail*, "New Discovery by Doreva Golda," February 11, 1937, page 22.
48 *The Globe and Mail*, "Doreva Prepares for Resumption," June 28, 1938, page 21.
49 *The Globe and Mail*, "Doreva Gold Mines given New Life," September 16, 1939, page 21.
50 *The Globe and Mail*, "Doreva Takes on Oil Properties," July 8, 1938, page 21.
51 A.E. Dawson, unpublished letter to Lynda Dawson, April 5, 1941.

Big Master Consolidated Mines

A.E. Dawson & Company went out on a limb for the Big Master mines in the Kenora District of Ontario. The Dawson ads promised "An extremely bright future,"[52] and "A Gold Mining Venture of Unusual Merit."[53] Some of the larger ads included mail-in coupons for information or to actually buy stock, and details of the mine's workings and ore prospects. Other security companies also offered the stock at the same time.[54] The mine had been worked around the turn of the century, then closed due to "financial troubles."[55] (The mine closed despite a "mild winter so far," with no blizzards and nothing colder than forty below zero.)

By 1936, with financing from Murwood Gold Mines, the mine was getting "encouraging results" in exploratory assays.[56] [57] Ernest placed at least six display ads—a full-court press—to sell securities for the venture. However, newspaper articles never subsequently reported actual gold production from the mine. It may have changed names, but, like so many other gold mine prospects, it simply disappeared from the written record. It was another legitimate mining gamble that apparently did not pan out for Ernest.

Depleted Mines

Ruby Queen Silver Mines

Ernest never actually advertised this mine, but he listed himself as a director of the mine in the Canadian *Who's Who* of 1936–37.[58] If nothing else, this citation showed that Ernest may have had good standing in the Canadian business community at that time.

Ruby Silver was apparently an Idaho project. Being a director sounded pretty good. However, I did not find the actual mine cited anywhere. One

---

52 *The Globe and Mail*, display ad, May 1, 1936, page 13.
53 *The Globe and Mail*, display ad, March 31, 1936, page 14.
54 Ibid.
55 *The Globe and Mail*, "Big Master Mine Closed," January 23, 1904, page 28.
56 *The Globe and Mail*, "Big Master Getting Encouraging Results," March 29, 1936, page 14.
57 *The Globe and Mail*, "Results Encouraging on Big Master Claims, March 12, 1936, page 15.
58 *The Canadian Who's Who of 1936-1937*.

related area was well-known for silver mining in Idaho. The Ruby Silver mine, if it existed, was in the area somewhere near Silver City, Idaho's location for gold and silver placer[59] and quartz vein resources. They were discovered near War Eagle Mountain in the 1860s.[60] The area was mined intensively, peaking in the 1880s. By World War II, mines in the area were pretty much mined out or depleted. During the forties, just after Dawson boasted of his association, only small-scale mining continued there. Today, Silver City is a mining ghost town on the National Register of Historic Places.

Ruby Queen appears to be a mine that looked good on paper, but in reality, was probably just a small, depleted mine at best, with little real potential.

Mines Linked to Fraud

Wylie-Dominion Gold Mines

The same 1936–1937 *Who's Who* listed Ernest again as a director, this time of Wylie-Dominion Gold Mines in Manitoba. Only one article about this company appears in the *Globe*.[61] According to the report, a court injunction prevented Wylie-Dominion from selling its property to Noranda Mines Limited, due to a lawsuit against the directors of the company. The suit, which was grounds for the injunction preventing the sale, was brought by the company's prospectors and shareholders.

The charges in the lawsuit were serious. "Statement of claim in the suit charges that $157,616.75 obtained from the sale of stock in the company by Capital Interests Limited has never been paid into the company treasury; that stock was unlawfully issued, and that directors [including Ernest] were unlawfully elected." The plaintiffs demanded an accounting of the company's fund, the return to the treasury of unlawfully issued stock, and that the court determine who the lawful directors of the company were.

Eventual outcomes of the lawsuit and the injunction were not reported in the *Globe*. In fact, no other mention of Wylie-Dominion ever appeared in

---

59   Placer gold is particulate gold found in glacial or alluvial sands. *Canadian Dictionary of the English Language*, ITP Nelson, Toronto,1997, page 1048.
60   Wikipedia, the Free Encyclopedia, .wikipedia.org'wiki'Silver-City,-Idaho June 6, 2021.
61   *The Globe and Mail*, "Injunction is Granted Against Wylie Dominion," August 26, 1935, page 13.

the paper. Thus, it is not known what Ernest's role as (unlawful) director was in the financial shenanigans. It does not look good, however. One wonders what happened to the $157,000 if they did not go to the treasury of the company? Did the directors pocket the funds? This looks like a textbook example of mining fraud in that era. It is the first solid indicator that Ernest was involved in unlawful or unethical conduct. It also shows that he was part of a financial community where fraud was an acceptable phenomenon.

Chappie-Mammoth Gold Mines

With Chappie-Mammoth Gold Mines, we meet a mining company that was actually named, with Ernest Dawson and John Forbes Woolcott, as a co-defendant in the U.S. Securities fraud indictments. The company appeared only twice in *Globe* articles. The first is a short note in a column on mining developments.[62] The article announced the formation of Chappie-Mammoth Gold Mines, located in Whitney Township in Ontario. (Whitney Township no longer exists, but the town of Whitney lies near the entrance to Algonquin Park.) Chappie-Mammoth was taking over the interests of Mammoth Porcupine Syndicates, apparently. The company had an announced value of three million shares, of which a little over one million were exchanged for the property. Of the remainder, 250,000 shares were said to be sold to finance diamond drilling at the 22,000-to-10,000-foot depths.

The word "Porcupine" was enough to hint that the property may have been associated with a famous northern Ontario gold rush region, Canada's largest gold-producing area to date.[63] Located near present-day Timmins, the gold rush field was discovered in 1911 and rapidly developed during the 1910s. A second wave of mines opened in the late 1920s and early 1930s, thanks to the low labour costs of the Great Depression and higher gold prices. Formerly ignored sites were developed during the 1940s and overall production peaked during the 1940s and 1950s.

---

62 *The Globe and Mail*, "McKinley Securities Show book value Over $1 a Share," October 18, 1934, page 14.
63 *Wikipedia, The Free Encyclopedia*, https://en.m.wikipedia.org "Porcupine Gold Rush." June 6, 2021.

The Porcupine gold rush, along with the Cobalt Silver Rush and the Kirkland Lake Gold Rush, was responsible for most of the settlement of northern Ontario.

According to *Globe* coverage of U.S. and Canadian indictments, Chappie-Mammoth was one of three corporations "allegedly controlled by Dawson."[64] The court documents characterized these stocks as "worthless." The only mention of Chappie-Mammoth, outside its mention in the U.S. indictments, was a tiny, anonymous *Globe* classified ad trying to locate Chappie-Mammoth stocks. The venture does not appear in listed or unlisted stock quotes or routine mining development news.

An adjoining property claim, McDougall-Porcupine Mines Ltd., was formed to conduct diamond drilling.[65] This suggests that Chappie-Mammoth, at one time, may have been an actual mining property. A final notice appeared in the *Globe* of Chappie-Mammoth's "surrender of its charter in 1945."

My conclusion about Chappie-Mammoth is that it may have been, at first, a real property, but became a legal shell for selling or switching stock, as indicated in the U.S. indictments. Promoters no doubt mentioned that it was associated with, in vague terms, the enormous Porcupine ore body, thus selling the worthless stock by virtue of its address alone.

---

64 *The Globe and Mail,* "Stock Fraud Charge Probed," December 5, 1942, page 5.
65 *The Globe and Mail,* "Unlisted Mines News quotations," November 21, 1936, page 25.

Leslie Y. Dawson

A.E. Dawson & Co. advertised heavily on the financial pages of many Canadian newspapers. This ad appeared March 7, 1936, in The Toronto Daily Star, on page 15.

CHAPTER 11:
The Ontario Operations

One day, a large, brown envelope arrived at my desk from Ontario Archives. It promised materials that could fill in information about the years missing from Grandad's wooden trunk. I hoped they might tell what this slightly sleazy stocks promoter was doing during the late 1930s. Imagine my shock, then, when the stack of papers revealed the disturbing details of Ernest's clearly illegal activities from 1940 through 1942.

Receiving the material from the Ontario Archives proved a turning point for me. No longer could I view my grandfather as just a slightly sleazy character. This was now a man who had actual victims, people who lost their hard-earned life savings—men and women who had to face old age penniless, with nothing to support them any longer.

I was angry then and plunged into my research with greater vigour than ever. And I ignored my sister, who suggested that Grandad himself was the victim of greedy investors who deserved what they got. The Archives painted quite a different picture. This was the family secret that had been hidden for two generations.

Gone was the shady mining-stock securities dealer, merely selling questionable mine stock that never produced, or mined-out properties in mined-out ore bodies. This was not a man who might, himself, have been the victim of dishonest prospectors or mining developers.

The envelope included legal documents from the Ontario Securities Commission (OSC) that showed Ernest Dawson to be an out-and-out thief, a man who persuaded retired farmers, teachers, and nurses to turn over their hard-earned cash and blue-chip stocks and bond certificates. He sold these stocks and deposited their profits into his own account. In exchange, he gave his clients stock certificates in his worthless shell companies—fictitious companies that he had recently invented out of whole cloth. He must have printed brochures about these companies, with fictional financial records. One company he claimed had been in business for decades. He placated his clients occasionally with imaginary dividends from these shell companies, giving them the veneer of genuine operations.

In October 1940, Ernest was once again making house calls in Toronto and rural and small-town Ontario. This time, however, it was not to sell insurance, but securities, and reminiscent of his early days selling insurance to farmers in north-central Ontario. He knew these people well. They were the salt of the earth, whom he'd written about in his short stories. They were, no doubt, impressed by this older, white-haired gentleman, well dressed and with a deep, reassuring voice, well-known in the Toronto business world. As he explained the latest trends in investment, he became familiar with their worries, their available cash, and their financial needs. He, too, had once been a farm worker, and admired their ability to save for their old age. He inquired about their savings, their stocks and bonds, acquired over the years. And he told them that he might have an even better deal for them!

A Con Game at Best

A successful confidence game requires that the victim cooperate with the confidence artist, consciously or unconsciously. Ernest's victims did just that. The victims share some personality characteristics:[66] they are more gullible, more trusting, more impulsive. They like to fantasize, and are somewhat greedy. Often they are going through a major life change—such as retirement—and are anxious about debt. In the context of major life changes, victims can become less stable, taking greater risks than they would ordinarily. Maria Konnikova says that risk takers, in one study, are six times more likely to fall victim to fraud. In such circumstances,

---

66 Konnikova, Maria, *The Confidence Game, Why We Fall for It… Every Time,* Viking, New York, 2016, page 46.

schemes or propositions that would look absurd in another light suddenly seem more attractive... Suddenly, something that once seemed like a gamble looks awfully appealing. A victim isn't necessarily foolish or greedy. A victim is simply more emotionally vulnerable at the exact moment the confidence artist approaches.

Much of the information in this chapter comes from the files of the OSC and the Ontario attorney general. The documents were used to support Canada's request for the later *extradition of A.E. Dawson, John Woolcot Forbes, and C.W.C. Perry* from the United States to Canada. These extradition requests were submitted to U.S. authorities in 1942 to show that the three men's crimes in Canada were also offences covered by the then current U.S / Canada extradition treaties. The files are currently in the Archives of Ontario.

Ernest and his team were good at identifying vulnerable people. For instance, Ernest made frequent visits to Bertha Hodgson and her husband in the Jarvis area of Toronto. He was probably a welcome visitor, and Mrs. Hodgson likely put the kettle on, made tea, and rustled up some cookies or homemade cake. Perhaps, as Ernest sat back and lit up his pipe, Mr. Hodgson offered a glass of sherry to their distinguished guest. After all, it wasn't often that a member of Toronto's business elite paid a visit. (And they probably did not know that the Ontario Securities Commission had outlawed home visits to sell securities.) Like other fraud victims, the couple may have willingly shared useful information about their circumstances with Ernest.

Ernest persuaded Mrs. Hodgson to "buy" 5,000 shares of Abitibi, which still exists today under various names. Abitibi was a large pulp, paper, and power company then fighting foreclosure. Threats of foreclosure arose because of the late-depression business environment and low paper prices.[67] No doubt it was a good time to buy Abitibi, since its stock price was low. Mrs. Hodgson paid for her Abitibi stock by turning over to Ernest her legitimate blue-chip stock: twenty-five valuable Noranda and two hundred Teck-Hughes. These were big-name, producing companies. Noranda, a diversified mining and industrial stock, had already paid three dividends of $1 per share that year

---

67 *The Globe and Mail*, "Grave Repercussions of Abitibi Foreclosure Seen by Gordon Taylor," October 16, 1940, page 16.

and was Canada's third largest gold producer.[68] [69] Teck-Hughes, another gold-mining concern, was also making money, about thirty-five cents profit per share by that July.[70]

Ernest took Mrs. Hodgson's Noranda and Teck-Hughes stocks and sold them. However, he sold them on his own account, not hers. The OSC record[71] states that "At that time Mrs. Hodgson thought that A.E. Dawson & Company had bought the Abitibis for her and were holding them, on her account." As a matter of fact, the evidence shows that the original 5,000 Abitibis purchased by A.E. Dawson & Company "were never ear-marked for Mrs. Bertha Hodgson; never appropriated to her account; and at all times were dealt with as though they were A.E. Dawson's own securities."

The Teck-Hughes securities were also "disposed of" as A.E. Dawson & Company securities, instead of being held as her collateral. All told, between selling the Noranda and Teck-Hughes stocks, and a cheque for $763.70, A.E. Dawson made $2,640 on Mrs. Hodgson. That would be $44,880 today. Meanwhile, Mrs. Hodgson received a fictional letter indicating that he had bought the Abitibi for her.

By 1940, though, the Hodgson matter was unusual for Ernest. By that time, he rarely did the sales pitch himself, according to the OSC. Usually, his two salesmen did the fieldwork. One was the Australian con artist, John Woolcott Forbes. The other salesman was C.W.C. Perry, an Englishman. Perry and Forbes often worked together in the field and in almost all cases tried to market shares and debentures of Dawson's shell companies, in exchange for shares and bonds of real value and cash held by the client. Other times, they bought worthless shares for their clients at greatly exaggerated prices, took their legitimate stock, and pocketed the differences.

Ernest himself was somehow vulnerable to Forbes when they first met. In fact, Ernest wrote in a letter to Lynda that "I have in reality been in prison

---

68 *The Globe and Mail,* "Noranda Nets $2.31 Per Share for Half Year," August 1, 1940, page 15.
69 *The Globe and Mail,* "Noranda Ranks Third as Producer of Gold," February 21, 1941, page 19.
70 *The Globe and Mail,* "Teck-Hughes Profits for First Nine Months Are 35 Cents a Share," July 1, 1940, page 19.
71 *Archives of Ontario File No. 1250,* Department of Attorney-General for Ontario. "Memorandum for the Attorney General's Department, Ontario Securities Commission," November 13, 1942, page 4.

ever since Forbes first entered my office." Probably, Ernest had stepped onto the slippery slope of fraud already, perhaps taking smaller steps. As far back as his insurance days, he may have been manipulating the stock market. We don't know. Certainly, he had entered the grey world with his Wylie-Dominion dealings and his Chappie-Mammoth stocks.

What did Forbes offer Ernest? Greater earnings, when the cash-strapped Ernest desperately needed money? Relief from having to make the actual sales calls? An opportunity to broaden the scale of his operation? A foolproof way to hoodwink the victims? Or all the above? Or did he threaten to divulge damaging information about Ernest? Whatever it was, Ernest fell into the temptations presented by the experienced fraudster from Australia. Although probably not innocent, Ernest was probably vulnerable to Forbes.

It would be interesting to know how Ernest paid his salesmen. Possibly it was a percentage of the take, a commission of sorts.

The OSC later charged that the Dawson-Forbes-Perry team had defrauded at least seventy-two Ontario victims. Their stolen securities were valued from $100 to $62,000 each—up to 1.032 million in 2021 dollars.

We were unable to uncover much about the victims of the scam. According to the OSC, the victim who lost the most was Mrs. S.H. Blake, a widow living in Toronto. The others included three doctors, four or five nurses, and six schoolteachers (three of whom were pensioners). Two of the victims, the Nelles, may have been sisters. The rest of the seventy-two victims were farmers' families...

A typical victim was Mrs. Mabel Van Loon, who may have been an older, retired woman or a widow. Over an extended period, she turned over thousands of dollars worth of bonds and cash in exchange for worthless stock in the Dawson shell companies.

Clearly, Ernest and his salesmen aimed for unsophisticated investors like Mrs. Van Loon, often people who had invested carefully and wisely until the Dawson team came along. They probably invested in the Dawson shell companies only after high-pressure tactics had been applied—frequent home visits, telephone calls, and mailings over an extended period.

In several cases, said the OSC, practically all the victims' life savings were taken.

Forbes: An Independent Fraudster

Two accounts suggest that Forbes may have conducted some of his fraudulent activities independent of Ernest's operation.

The first indicator is a *Toronto Star* story[72] about Forbes's situation after his indictment in New York.

> John Woolcott Forbes, reputed to be worth $5,000,000 when his financial enterprises blew up in Australia, is wanted in Ontario to face stock fraud charges aggregating $150,000. Roy B. Whitehead, Ontario securities commissioner, said Forbes will be better remembered in Toronto as George Blake, not only by the people who bought his stock but by those who were guests at his lavish parties. John Woolcott Forbes is now in New York's House of Correction waiting trial on charges which could bring him 152 years' imprisonment if convicted. After that it will be a rush for who gets him next, Mr. Whitehead said. Australia has first claim. Charges against him there run into the millions. These followed the crash of his vast investment companies. Ontario securities commissioner has 10 informations against him. 'It is impossible to tell how many people lost money through dealings with him,' said Mr. Whitehead.

For some reason, this article never mentions Forbes's relationship with Ernest. This may be because the newspaper was simply protecting one of its favourite sons, or because these fraudulent activities were independent of the Dawson operation. Ernest and his wife, after all, appeared frequently on the *Star*'s society pages. They were involved with church and school affairs and were pillars of Toronto's upper crust. They lived in Rosedale. The *Star*, unlike the *Globe and Mail*, chose to protect their people, it appears.

The second suggestion of independent activity is an excerpt concerning a "Mr. X" from Christopher Armstrong's exhaustive history of the securities

---

72 *Toronto Daily Star*, "Ontario Seeks 'Second Ponzi' Awaiting Trial in New York," January 18, 1943.

industry of Canada.⁷³ While the dates of the story indicate that Mr. X was operating in Canada before 1940, the rest of the story does seem to jive with Forbes's activities.

> These inquiries revealed that the boiler rooms [share-selling phone banks] were being run by thoroughly shady types with long records of brushes with the authorities. In one instance a "Mr. X" had surfaced in Ontario in late 1933 and during the brief boom of 1934 had created a brokerage that employed over a hundred salesmen as well as a "tame" radio broadcaster. When the OSC [Ontario Securities Commission] became suspicious and seized the firm's books, it was discovered that X was a principal of the company being promoted, which claimed to have a producing mine when in fact the property bore a sheriff's notice offering it for sale with no takers. Less than 15 percent of the funds raised from the public had ended up in the company treasury, and nothing had been spent upon development. Those who had endorsed the man for registration with the OSC proved to know little about his background, which included *previous legal problems in Australia and an outstanding warrant in Britain*. The British offence was not deemed serious enough to justify the expense of deportation, so the offender was simply stripped of his OSC registration and allowed to remain in Canada. After lying low for a year or so, he had applied for and been granted a new licence.

If the man was Forbes, this might have been the point at which he approached Ernest.

It is certainly not clear that Mr. X was, indeed, John Woolcott Forbes or George Blake. However, it would not be surprising to learn that he had international activities outside Australia. He certainly had enough money and the know-how to set up such a scheme.

---

73   Armstrong, Christopher, *Blue Skies and Boiler Rooms, Buying and Selling Securities in Canada 1870-1940*, University of Toronto Press, Toronto, 1997, page 268. The entry also references the *Financial Post*, January 30, 1937.

C.W.C. Perry: The Third Man

Charles Walter Cuthbert (C.W.C.) Perry played a role as a lesser, third co-conspirator in the A.E. Dawson stock fraud affairs. Born in England, he lived in Canada from 1910 onward—an immigrant Englishman of the same generation as Ernest. Of the three found guilty of security fraud charges, we know the least about Perry. He probably played a secondary role, however, to the smooth-talking John Woolcott Forbes.

But oh, what a tangled web of deceit Perry and his partners wove!

Newspaper accounts and the Ontario archival material indicate that Perry worked as a salesman for A.E. Dawson & Company. He apparently worked side by side with Forbes in the field. One case, beginning March 1, 1940, involved the victim Mrs. Mabel L. Van Loon of Waterford, Ontario. Waterford was a small, rural community southwest of Hamilton, today numbering only 3,100 people. Canadian authorities alleged that Perry was involved in another scheme. "A.E. Dawson & Company, chiefly through his salesmen, C.W.C. Perry and George Blake [John Woolcott Forbes], sold approximately 2495 shares of Equity Holding Corporation at approximately $5.00 a share, which cost them an average of $1.08 a share."[74] To make these sales, they would have had to misrepresent the true value of Equity Holding Corporation equities.

From the OSC account of Mrs. Van Loon's investments, she was victim of a long-standing, high-pressure campaign by Forbes and Perry, with front office backup from Ernest. The goal? To rob her of all her hard-earned, legitimate securities. They kept going back for more. Mrs. Van Loon was no doubt a naive investor, perhaps an older woman subject to the combined charms of the two salesmen. She was also reassured by the phony 7½ percent dividend cheques manufactured by Ernest.

---

74 *Ontario Securities Commission, Archives of Ontario file # 1250*, 1942, "Memorandum for the Attorney General's Department Re. A.E. Dawson, C.W.C. Perry, John Woolcott Forbes alias George Blake," November 13, 1942, page 8.

The Ontario Charges

In 1942 Ontario authorities charged Ernest and Forbes with seventeen offences.[75] Most listed Ernest as the sole defendant, while five also listed Forbes. Many of the charges named Ernest alone, I believe, because it was he who converted the stolen shares belonging to a victim into his own name, or into the assets of A.E. Dawson & Company.

Forbes was also charged with one count of forging signatures on securities turned over to him. This might have been a case of one thief (Forbes) robbing another thief (Ernest).

The Three-Part System: Switching, A Ponzi Scheme, and Misrepresentation

The overall pattern of the frauds was that Ernest, Forbes, and Perry persuaded investors to trade in thousands of dollars in cash, and even more in marketable securities. There were three possible methods of persuasion:

- First, in return, the victims received shares—this was called "switching"—in the various worthless shell companies that had been recently created by Ernest.
- Second, some were courted using phony "dividends." These were not based on company profits, but simply taken from money "invested" by later investors. (This made it a Ponzi scheme of sorts.) The dividends encouraged the victims to invest more.
- Thirdly, some bought worthless, shell company stocks at highly overvalued prices (the shell company stocks being, essentially, worthless). These shares were simply misrepresented as worth much more, with the operation pocketing the difference.

---

75   *Archives of Ontario, File No. 1250*, 1942, Department of Attorney-General for Ontario, "Warrant in the matter of the application for Extradition of A.E. Dawson and John Woolcott Forbes, alias George Blake" to the United States of America Southern District of New York, pages 4-6.

Many of the investors, such as the Nelles family (see Appendix B), had carefully built up sound, diversified portfolios. Others, with more modest budgets, had invested in mining penny stocks. The silver-tongued Dawson team apparently persuaded them to give up their sound blue chips for a complex fiction of shell companies.

The typical selling pattern in the 1930s was quite uniform. A report to the U.S. Securities and Exchange Commission[76] (SEC) describes the general approach:

> The victim was first solicited by mail, told of the great money-making possibilities of the mine or oil well involved and asked to merely send his name and address on a prepaid post card (no obligation) to be kept apprised of developments. Within a few days, the victim received a phone call (or possibly a further piece of sales literature or telegram and then the phone call). The fraud artist then talked about new and great discoveries or oil strikes or gold or other rare metal strikes (depending upon the then current promotion) giving glowing accounts of the status of the property or describing its proximity to someone else's great discovery. It was invariably hammered home that the victim must hurry--that the offering was below market or in advance of a public offering; or for a limited time only; or that only a limited number of shares were left at these ridiculously low prices. The victim was forever being let in on the ground floor. Of course, the shares were $1 par, fully paid, but with fast action could be had at only 70 cents each and of course the shares either just had been or soon would be listed on the stock exchange and they'd triple in price in a few days.

Were the victims just greedy individuals falling for a get-rich-quick scheme? It was much more complicated than that. First of all, without today's access to online information, it would be difficult for ordinary people to verify the claims of the salesmen. They would have to subscribe to a paper like the *Globe and Mail* and follow the stock market tables daily. There were no convenient online listings in those days, only the word of mouth of

---

76 *The Canadian Problem: Illegal Securities Offerings, 1933-1955*, Lund, A.H., U.S. Securities Exchange Commission, 1955, unpublished, page 22.

trusted people supposedly in the know. Furthermore, often the Dawson team efforts extended over aggressive, years-long campaigns, probably involving several visits, many cups of tea, various phony accounting statements and brochures (remember, Ernest was a writer), and even some real hooks—fictional "dividends" supposedly from earlier investments in the shell companies. Everything looked fine until the victims tried to get their hands on the money or the securities. Some had no idea they'd been plundered until the OSC investigation informed them. (Not knowing you've been cheated is the sign of a completely successful con job.) The frauds were sophisticated, patient, and designed around carefully built-up trust.

An Ancestor to Bernie Madoff?

In some ways, Ernest's set-up might have been an ancestor to the more recent Bernie Madoff Ponzi scheme of 1968. Madoff had an "affinity" scheme targeting well-heeled members of the Jewish community. Ernest's affinity group consisted of retirees, pensioners, and rural and small-town investors. Ernest and Madoff rarely met their investors personally—the salesmen did the work. Like Ernest, Madoff paid "dividends." Madoff's were around 10 percent. Ernest's were around 7 percent, also a good return. Both operations' dividends greatly enhanced their firms' credibility and motivation for additional investments. Ernest's salesmen delivered "dividends" to their victims in person, but went away with even more of their assets. The dividends were not, of course, based on real investment earnings, just a certain percentage of the take. Both Ernest and Madoff juggled funds, insider tips, and account statements to give the appearance of real investments with real dividends.

From the available documents, we do not know what finally tipped the OSC off about Ernest's operation. Certainly, they would have investigated the operations after they discovered that Blake was actually Forbes, a known fraudster. There may also have been complaints from one or more of the victims, after they tried to cash in or sell their securities. Whatever got the OSC started, it's clear from the existing documents that they went over the A.E. Dawson & Company books with a fine-toothed comb—and a good forensic accountant.

The OSC summary of the scheme suggests the government's exacting attempt to match securities conversions, client accounts, real stock values of the shell companies, and consultations with other securities dealers. Using all these methods, Ernest and his men were eventually (after they had been arrested by the United States authorities) charged with explicit fraudulent activities in Ontario.

One unknown factor is the extent to which Ernest involved his family in the scheme. More recently, Bernie Madoff used many family members as officers and representatives of his firm. One of Dawson's shell companies, Norco Thompson, featured Ernest's son Ken as a director. Ken Dawson, who was to become a respected banker in Toronto, may not have known anything—although that is unlikely--about his company's inflated stock values or its role as a shell company for A.E. Dawson & Company. Also, Grove (Lakefield) school records say that Harry was working "in his father's business." Some unsubstantiated Dawson family rumours suggest that Ernest's son Alan may also have been involved, although he would have been very young at the time.

The OSC typically seized entire records of suspected securities fraudsters. This was probably the time during which Ernest and his salesmen abruptly moved into the United States and set up shop in New York City.

A year or so later, when Ernest and company were in American custody, Ontario authorities requested his extradition, along with Forbes and Perry. The request listed the victims, the money, and the securities involved in the frauds. The team seemed to take every bit of cash and securities they could get their hands on—the list shows a remarkably thorough robbery of most victims.

The victims turned over a variety of securities, from mining penny stocks to rock-solid industrials. Dawson and company were not proud—they took them all. Keep in mind that the 1940 Canadian dollar was worth about 168 times a 2021 dollar. That would make Mrs. Blake's loss alone worth nearly $1 million today ($56,727 in 1940 dollars).

The totals for the fourteen counts would amount to just under $3 million today. That included $72,156 in cash and $25,950 in bonds, plus $31,000 in stock securities—or $129,106 all told, in 1940 dollars, just over $2 million 2021 dollars.

However, this figure accounts for the losses of just the people listed in the indictments—and just those losses that the OSC could prove. The OSC claimed that more than seventy people had been defrauded, not merely the fourteen people listed in the charges. The total fraud activity certainly amounted to millions more.

Ernest's activities at the time amounted to large-scale white-collar crime. And he was just getting started on operations in the United States.

CHAPTER 12:
The Canadian Problem

Nothing has suggested that Ernest knew the technical aspects of mining, about gold and silver, or drilling for oil... but suddenly, in 1934, he advertised as a specialist in this field. What he did know was stocks. He knew how to buy low and sell high. He knew how to make money by buying stocks on the margin. No doubt he'd played a pivotal role in investing the millions of Toronto Casualty's funds. He probably thought he could read engineers' reports about mines. And while he could probably be fooled by mining engineers and geological reports, he knew how to play the stock game.

Mining stocks had been a rough-and-tumble field since the 1920s. Ernest was, no doubt, aware of fraudulent practices among securities dealers at that time. He may have read an article describing one such practice, "switching," in the *Financial Post*.[77] "Stock swindles and high-pressure salesmen have developed misuse of the telephone in their operations... In Canada these operations are generally what are termed 'switchers'. They call a person holding some good marketable stock and try to get possession in exchange for some worthless security... made use of the long-distance telephone to interest suburbanites of moderate means in stock transactions. They assured their customers they would net large profits in a short time, it is charged." Indeed, this article describes the *modus operandi* used by Ernest in later years.

---

77 *The Financial Post*, "Stock Swindlers Using the Phone, New York Takes Action in Courts to Curb Activities," April 24, 1925.

Fraud Commonplace in Market

Fraud was rampant in mining and oil stocks for decades. The problem lasted well into the 1950s. For example, on November 4, 1954, no fewer than two articles on Canadian stock fraudsters appeared on the same page. In one, two Montreal stock salesmen were wanted in Detroit for a $300,000 stock swindle. They were arrested by the RCMP on a U.S. grand jury indictment. In the other,[78] two Canadians used a phony television production to bait Hollywood elite with "worthless uranium and television stocks." The uranium firm sold stock at fifty cents a share to develop uranium deposits in Saskatchewan. No uranium had ever been found in the company holdings.

Fraud occurred on large and small scales. Everyone was doing it, apparently. For instance, in 1942, a small-time operator was sentenced in stock fraud[79] of $250. He was sentenced to a two-year suspended sentence to "facilitate restitution measures."

Stock sales were most often accompanied by high-pressure telephone sales calls. Ontario's attorney general complained in 1945 of receiving twenty-nine calls from Toronto investment firms in January of that year. The *Star* printed an editorial[80] bemoaning the bad reputation Ontario was experiencing, thanks to stock fraud.

"It is rather serious," an expert was quoted, "when you think you are investing $1,800 in a promising mine in the belief that most of it will go into development and then find that only 30 cents actually reaches the property, and the balance remains with the optionee or underwriter." The editorial noted that Better Business Bureau executives at New York warned U.S. investors against putting their money into "wildcat" mining shares being offered by promoters in Canadian cities, especially Toronto. They declared that

> Canadian mining stock swindling has reached such proportions that agencies in both Canada and the United States, charged with protecting investors, are greatly concerned... These men will victimize Canadians just as quickly as they will victimize Americans—and they should not be permitted to victimize

---

78   *The Toronto Daily Star*, "Charge 2 Canadians in Stock Fraud, Used Movie Stars' Names," November 4, 1954.
79   *The Toronto Daily Star*, "Stock Promoter Jailed," January 4, 1942.
80   *The Toronto Daily Star*, "Stop the Racketeers," Editorial, June 16, 1945.

anybody. They should not be permitted to ruin Canada's good name, to say nothing of the good name of honest brokerage houses whose reputation is injured by the misdeeds of the dishonest one.

Ernest developed his game using his considerable charm, his good character reputation, and whatever props served the purpose. Buried in his big wooden trunk, certain artifacts caught my imagination immediately. The first was a trio of geological maps that seemed connected to his new field. The three are full-sized maps of southern British Columbia, published by the Province of British Columbia, one dated May 1, 1940. The maps are folded, re-folded, and worn, as if they had been opened and discussed many times, perhaps with prospective clients/investors. Ernest never advertised a B.C. mine, but clearly he was involved in selling some related stocks. One of the maps was for prospectors, with known mineral finds marked in different areas. Ernest had circled in pencil a large area west and south of Prince George, with small circles along the Nechako River. Perhaps the circled areas were mineral claims or areas of exploration by a particular mining company or prospector. Another map shows surveyed areas available for sale in the Cariboo, along the Goat River, near McBride. Two of the maps include printed comments in red italics. One read, "Numerous bars and benches on Fraser River and tributaries are since discovery, one of the important sources of placer gold particularly between Soda Creek and Prince George. Occasional platinum." And near Goat River, "The Barkerville area has been the most productive Placer GOLD fields in B.C. And still presents a good field for prospectors."

These worn maps no doubt impressed potential stock customers eager for the promise of riches. The maps must have been some of Ernest's sales tools. To the naive investor, they had the look of authenticity, published by the government, useful in a sales pitch.

Mining Stocks Popular Investments Despite Fraud

Eager and naive investors were common in those decades. In fact, an entire business culture and industry had evolved on Bay Street to accommodate their needs. These investors were people who accepted the fact that Canadian mining stocks were, indeed, highly risky. The mines were known to be more likely to fail than to bring in actual dividends. It was accepted that mining stocks, were essentially, a form of high-stakes gambling. Buying penny stocks in a mine was like buying a lottery ticket today. Nonetheless, they were "hot" investments in the thirties and forties since they could also deliver untold riches if the mine in question proved productive.

One needs only to look at newspapers of the time. The *Globe and Mail* offered updates on mines and regular columns assessing their progress. The *Toronto Daily Star* kept readers up to date on fraud, but also reported on mining affairs. The *Financial Post* did too. There were also mining newsletters, with all the latest insider information. All papers printed large display ads for mining stock. For instance, a single page where an A.E. Dawson & Company ad appeared in the *Globe* was accompanied by prominent display ads for *nine* other mines or mining security brokers. Newspaper ads often included maps, details of exploration, progress on actual digging and rock sampling, and mining engineers' reports. While most of the ads were understated, many suggested that the stock was, at present, "undervalued"—buy now and sell later when the price of the stock rose. Others promised that the mine in question was "about to go into actual gold production"—a thinly veiled promise of dividends, and riches.

Ernest was sometimes caught up in a spectacular failure, such as when the Kirkam Scanion & Company lost its licence to sell securities in 1936. A.E. Dawson & Company was among the nearly one hundred clients that lost money. The *Globe* termed the situation as a "debacle"[81] and listed forty creditors and claims, and more than forty-one brokers to which Kirkam owed money. A.E. Dawson did not lose much, but other companies such as Bell Telephone and The Canadian Bank of Commerce lost hundreds and thousands. "In regards to the heavier losses, it is learned that these have been largely cleaned up by the brokerage houses themselves, so that clients have not had to suffer," reported the *Globe*. In other words, the brokers ate the losses.

---

81 *The Globe and Mail*, "Kirkham Creditors Will Meet May 27 to Appoint Trustee. Claims Settled With Company's Clients," May 19, 1936.

U.S. and Canadian Authorities Act

The organization that was most aware and concerned with Canadian stock fraud was the U.S. Securities Exchange Commission—the SEC. In fact, the SEC put a name on the phenomenon; they called it *The Canadian Problem*. A confidential staff report summarizes the U.S. headaches with Canadian fraud in a 1955 history by A.H. Lund. The report describes the continuing business and law enforcement milieu on both sides of the border, and the frustrations the U.S. government had in bringing Canadian fraudsters to account.

A similar perspective, but from the Canadian authorities' side, is offered by Christopher Armstrong in his financial history, *Blue Skies and Boiler Rooms: Buying and Selling Securities in Canada, 1870-1940*.

The SEC report begins with a broad picture of mining securities:

> The money which developed American [and Canadian] industry and commerce came largely from the sale of securities by or on behalf of the promoters and pioneering corporations responsible for such developments. On occasion people were urged to buy securities in corporations which outwardly also appeared to be honestly managed, only to learn later that the representations made at the time of sale were untrue and that fraud had taken place. Unscrupulous securities promoters and enterprises were often indistinguishable from the honest promoter and enterprise. Certain states about 45 years ago began to develop forms of securities legislation to protect their citizens. The Canadian provinces followed closely in enacting similar protective legislation.

The various state and provincial legislative attempts to curb securities fraud were called "blue sky" laws. They were enacted to prevent financial pirates from selling "everything in the state except the blue sky." Despite their intent, blue sky laws were largely ineffective and inconsistent, with weak enforcement. State and provincial attempts to legislate remained lenient enough to still attract securities businesses within their borders. Canadian lawmakers did not want laws that dampened the capitalization of their resource industries, such as mines.

One *Financial Post* article described the general laissez-faire attitude towards regulation in Canada.

there have been certain industrial offerings in recent years, the literature of which contained quite a lively flights of fancy as any mining prospectus, and the public fell for them just as readily. And now, just when the gentlemen who are skilled in such productions are getting into their stride there is talk of a blue sky law... *The public does not want to be bothered with any grandmotherly regulations; [my italics]* all it needs is such regulations that a man can definitely figure the chances as he can in roulette, if he wants to risk his money that way.

Note that in Canada, the *provinces,* not the federal government, developed the anti-fraud legislation. In fact, noted the Lund report, "The Dominion of Canada has not enacted any types of securities laws comparable to our [U.S.] Federal securities laws." This single fact was to cause no end of frustrations to the American securities authorities, said Lund.

In 1933 and 1934, the U.S. enacted sweeping laws protecting investors from securities fraud. The 1933 law required full disclosure about securities being offered. The Securities Exchange Act of 1934 regulated the secondary trading of securities through brokers or dealers. It also established the Securities Exchange Commission (SEC) to enforce the acts. Millions of dollars were made and lost each year through trading in the secondary market, with brokers like Ernest acting between the companies and investors. The 1934 act extended all requirements to securities traded in the secondary market. Provided that the company had more than a certain number of shareholders and a certain amount of assets, the act required that issuers regularly file company information (including risk factors) with the SEC. The law also required that brokers be registered with the SEC. Conducting fraud was also illegal if the broker or company used the United States mail system to communicate a fraud. This stipulation was to bring down Ernest and his henchmen.

When the 1934 SEC law was enacted, Canada, with no federal laws, loomed as the happy hunting ground for salesmen, brokers, dealers, and mail fraud artists. No federal Canadian laws covered inter-provincial or international commerce, including long-distance telephone calls. (Toronto brokers operated huge phone banks making calls to Canadian and American investors.) The provinces apparently had no more jurisdiction outside their own borders than an individual state did in the U.S. Initially, great numbers of American securities salesmen migrated to Toronto and Montreal. However, those going to Montreal met with vigorous enforcement by the Quebec authorities. Thus Toronto—and Bay Street—became the securities fraud mecca for U.S. and Canada. In Ontario, securities fraud was tacitly tolerated and immune from prosecution by the U.S.

The problem was described by a frustrated writer of a *Toronto Star* article.[82] The article noted,

> Gold works magic everywhere, but never better than it does for the Toronto promoters of worthless mining stock who are getting busy again, this time in Texas.
>
> Complaints have been reaching the securities and exchange commission but the story is an old one and the answer is the same. As long as the promoters stay in Canada, the S.E.C. is stymied.
>
> Only an extradition treaty the commission said today in its annual report to Congress, can put a halt to the fraud practiced on U.S. investors by a "numerically small group" of Canadian promoters "in willful violation" of American securities laws.
>
> The Texans whose complaints are being heard now, and thousands of Americans before them, have been sold worthless stock in gold and uranium mines and in oil promotions, but because the offenders stay in Canada, they are safe from U.S. prosecution.
>
> The commission has constantly warned American investors against offers made from Toronto and in its report to Congress said that the "fringe group of stock promoters operating out of Toronto" is in no way "representative of the vast majority of persons engaged in the securities business in Canada."
>
> "Nevertheless," the report stated, "the activities of these offenders have resulted in extremely large dollar losses to U.S. investors."

---

82 *The Toronto Daily Star,* United Press, March 6, circa 1942.

The article noted that a proposed 1941 extradition treaty was allowed to die by the Canadian Parliament, and that without such a treaty the SEC could not bring fraudsters to justice. This was a clearly political move. Many Canadians resisted the idea of an extradition treaty on patriotic grounds. Such a treaty would enable American control over Canadian affairs, thus threatening Canadian sovereignty. Thus, Parliament allowed the treaty to die, only to be revived in later years.

In 1949,[83] the Canadian government was still not contemplating federal jurisdiction over stock fraud. The government was content to leave such regulations to the provinces, unlike the federal involvement in the United States.

Today, the Canadian federal government is still considering the matter of a national stock market supervisory law. Report after report has recommended such a move over the years, but national laws are still being debated. In 2021 provinces still operate separately in securities regulation.

Mining Stocks: Legitimate Fundraisers or Fraud?

Part of the problem in the 1930s and 1940s was the very nature of the mining business. As one witness to the SEC reported,

> Small investors like a gamble, but it [the proposed SEC legislation] does what all legislation of that kind does… it makes it practically impossible to get speculative venture capital because you see once you say you are going to protect the small investor, then almost the first thing you say is that we must make quite sure that when he invests he gets something real, something substantial, but a mining venture in its early days is not real and is not substantial. It is a hope and a prospect. As soon as you pass legislation such as the SEC, you have virtually stopped that kind of investment because you have said to little investors, "We are not going to let you put your money into gambles of that kind."

Ernest, starting out as a mining securities broker, probably trod a fine line between selling stocks for legitimate mining capitalizations and the more questionable stock offerings. Indeed, in both the U.S. and Canada, natural

---

83 *The Winnipeg Tribune*, "Canada Unlikely to Clamp Down on Stock Frauds," July 18, 1949.

resource development blurred these lines considerably. Looking back in 1955, Lund's report summarizes the issues thusly:

> Canada with its vast untapped natural resources has been described as the "last frontier". New industrial plants, the development of hydro-electric power, dams, roads, railroads, oils and minerals require large amounts of capital. There is a ready American market for products and materials which come from the mines and forests of Canada. The biggest investors in these enterprises are the Canadians themselves. The U.S. public has supplied the major portion of foreign capital. The moneys which have been siphoned off in fraudulent promotions are needed for legitimate Canadian enterprises. While the U.S. investor is willing to take a chance he should know what sort of chance he is taking and that the gamble is an honest gamble, that the cards are not marked and the dice loaded. A chance to assess a risk must be afforded to investors. We must do everything possible to ensure that Americans who put their capital to work will be secure in the knowledge that they will be dealt with fairly and that their risks will be informed risks.

Canadian and American investors were ripe for the picking by unscrupulous, high-pressure dealers, despite constant consumer warnings by authorities. In Canada, resource development was an important engine for economic growth, especially in the field of mining. Investors were told that the little guys often came up with fabulous finds in unexpected and remote places. Because investors wanted access to these operations in their early stages, Canadian provincial governments often took the approach of self-regulation by brokers in the stock exchanges.[84] Needless to say, self-regulation often resulted in conflict of interest, insider trading, and other abuses. The foxes were guarding the hen house. Stock market regulation was ineffective; furthermore, in regulating off-the-floor trading, stocks traded "on the street."

From the 1920s through the 1950s, Canadians and Americans in all walks of life plunged enthusiastically into stock speculation, especially in mining shares.[85] After the market crash of 1929, however, Ontario created

---

84 Armstrong, Christopher, *Blue Skies and Boiler Rooms, Buying and Selling Securities in Canada, 1870 to 1940*, University of Toronto Press, Toronto, 1997, pages 5-6.
85 *Ibid*, page 7

the Ontario Securities Commission (OSC). It was Canada's first specialized tribunal for the regulation of securities trading. Bay Street was the epicentre of mining stock activity. The OSC required registrations of brokers and salesmen to eliminate fraudsters, and granted the government special powers to investigate and prosecute them. Ultimately, Ernest and his partners had to face indictments from the OSC.

Fraud was rampant on Canadian stock markets. For example, one 1930 article[86] listed ten stockbrokers who were indicted in Toronto for conspiracy to defraud. In addition, that same day, four brokerage houses had their files seized by the OSC and two mining stocks had to cease trading. Another article, typical of the day, was a 1937 piece[87] that cited a mining securities firm as being charged for misleading the public about stock values and trading activity.

Years later, in 1954, the same conditions operated in Canada. Keith Funsten, president of the New York Stock Exchange, denounced the "shoddy shysters" and "rat hole salesmen" operating out of Canada.[88] He said that many promoters pocketed the money they collected in stock sale, without investing in the development of the mining properties. "Suckers are their gold mine."

Evidence suggests, as the reader will see, that Ernest offered both "an honest gamble" along with several fraudulent promotions. He did both, in Ontario and later in New York City.

Ernest Honestly Seeking Resources

On the one hand, Ernest's letters to his wife Lynda describe a businessman deeply into the resource business, in this case oil and Mexican timber. A California venture seemed to be an honest attempt to produce an actual product, oil. He tells Lynda about the exploratory oil well operation in California and a prospective timber deal in Mexico.[89]

He wrote,

---

86   *Nanaimo Daily News,* "Ten Representatives of Stock Brokerage Houses Arrested,", January 30, 1930.
87   *The Ottawa Journal,* "Securities' Firm Faces Charge," August 4, 1937.
88   *The Progress,* "Operation Sucker," November 1954, page 12.
89   Dawson, Ernest, personal communications, letter to Lynda Dawson, October 10, *circa* 1940, Guadalupe, Mexico.

If we can get financing, which appears likely, I shall be alright. Am hoping I shall be able to get into actual production by the middle of December. If all goes well then start to recover.

The news I got... of the well was highly promising, but only oil will make an oil well, so I will await results before again letting myself go off the deep end. The same amount of money, spent on my timber deal... will have... the whole family in a prospective business for generations.

From this letter, we can infer that Ernest had invested a great deal of money and had, perhaps, gambled his wealth and "gone off the deep end." Subsequent letters never mention actually striking oil. In a letter[90] from the U.S. prison in later years, Ernest reflected on his bad luck in the resource business. He mused that he was relieved to no longer be worrying over these matters, which could have been solved, he felt, with a single stroke of good luck. A gambler's explanation.

As evidence of his honest efforts, he points ironically to the modest contents of his trunk, which was shipped home from Mexico after his 1942 arrest. He asserts that when he did make money, he re-invested it in his company's operations rather than living a conspicuously wealthy lifestyle.

They [the trunk contents] are mute witnesses to my career of wild extravagances and self indulgence. Not a new article amongst them, indeed not an item of exterior clothing not almost too shabby for wear. In my night club life, my drinking, my dissipation—generally not a penny, except for tobacco and the odd movie. My family spending has never exceeded the quite modest figure of the most modest establishment on our street where we have lived for over twenty years. What money I have made, and it has at times been substantial, has gone back into the channels of my business for the benefit of my clients generally who are the shareholders of the various companies in which I and they have been interested. Putting money into development work for the hoped for benefit of all instead of salting it away as most of my ilk in my business

---

90 Dawson, Ernest, personal communications, letter to Lynda Dawson from prison, December 19, 1942.

do, buying back stock sold to clients and keeping on facing a downward trend that led eventually to the chaos of war and utter ruin. I should like to think you get this picture accurately. I have of course no fear of your loyalty and support, but I want your head to be able to confirm your heart. When I reflect upon the absence of any splash whatever in the raising of our admittedly fine family this absence of any social glitter. Estrangement living, not as much as a motor boat at the lake or a golf club for the family notwithstanding the fact that any member of our family is acceptable in any respectable family group of our fairly wide acquaintance, and further reduce this argument to what you and I have actually spend upon ourselves, well the barren state of your jewelry box and my wardrobe give the answer. I have no qualms of conscience commensurable with my present state of affairs. I understand the 'Telegram' to give color to its news item, referred to my 'palatial residence in Rosedale.' It is by no means palatial but it affords for a lusty group of Dawsons, as many happy memories as any house of its character in the city.

On the other hand, the list of Ernest's gold mine securities offers an incomplete but telling record of non-producing, exhausted, and simply bad or illegal mines. His poor record suggests that as a mining securities broker, he simply wasn't very good. This struggle may have moved him, by the end of the 1930s, to try his hand at outright fraud. He may have found straightforward fraud—as so many of his fellow stockbrokers did—easier than trying to predict the fickle outcomes of investing in mines and oil wells. And since so many of his fellow Toronto brokers were involved in fraud, he seems to have decided to join them.

CHAPTER 13:
Partner in Crime: John Woolcott Forbes

John Woolcott Forbes slipped into Canada without setting off any alarm bells. Nobody knew that he was an internationally wanted criminal from Australia, wanted for multi-million-pound fraud. Nobody knew that he had escaped to India, was captured, and jumped bail, or that he'd briefly shown up in England.

No, he came to Toronto with a new name and a new persona. He was George Blake and soon became known for lavish Toronto parties. Somewhere along the way, he met Ernest Dawson, and they talked.

Forbes played a significant role in the Ernest Dawson story. Apparently, Ernest blamed Forbes for much of his subsequent legal trouble. I was unable to find any record of how they came to work together—just that Forbes walked into Ernest's office one day, and the die was cast. They worked together in Ontario, in New York City, and possibly in Mexico. It was a long association, and both men blamed the other for their eventual fall from grace. What is clear, however, is that they made an effective team in conducting stock fraud in at least two countries, with Forbes working the "marks" in person, and Ernest playing a behind-the-scenes role as financier and corporate organizer.

Changing names was not new for Forbes. In 1904, he was born of Italian parents under the baptismal name of Luis Benevenuto Brandi. Socially ambitious, he anglicized his name in Australia.[91] He lived near Woolcott and Forbes streets in suburban Sydney, Australia, and from that invented the name John Woolcott Forbes, which he legally acquired. Using his new name, he worked his way into Australia's social and financial elite.

Forbes told people[92] that he had grown up on a million-acre sheep-ranching station somewhere in Australia. On the other hand, Murray Guy Smith, in a court deposition, testified that he had known Forbes as a jackaroo. Jackaroos were sort of ranching interns at a cattle or sheep ranch. Smith testified that Forbes had worked on a northwest station in Western Australia thirty years before, and that he had changed his name.

Forbes worked his way up from the agricultural world to the big cities of southeast Australia. There he became a financier and the biggest celebrity in Australia, according to many news accounts.[93] His press coverage is reminiscent of Donald Trump's recent status. One 1938 article[94] called him a "spectacular financier," as well as having a "Midas touch in business."

In another newspaper account,[95] Forbes was

> recognized as a genius of finance and better known in racing circles as the "Bullfighter," which sobriquet he earned by his colossal wagering on Sydney and Melbourne race tracks some years ago. The high pressure financier who has become a romantic and colorful personality in Australia and is the owner... of perhaps the most magnificent modern mansion in Australia—a residence recently mentioned as a suitable home next year for the Duke and Duchess of Kent.

The Aussie press followed every move of Forbes's life. The press played the role as an adoring pack. Nearly everything he did was deemed newsworthy. One article even noted when he placed a mere one pound bet on an obscure

---

91 *Toronto Daily Star,* "Ontario Seeks 'Second Ponzi' Awaiting Trial in New York," January 18, 1943.
92 *Singleton Argus,* "Glad to go to Australia again," November 2, 1942.
93 A search under the name "John Woolcott Forbes" in Australian digital archives yields nearly ten thousand "hits" in small and large publications.
94 *Truth,* "Woolcott Forbes Left With Tram Fare," February 6, 1938.
95 *Truth,* "£36,000 Will Be Paid, Says Woolcott Forbes," November 27, 1938, page 21.

horse, in contrast to the thousands he sometimes wagered. Another article concerned the cost of carpets in his mansion.

Things turned sour in 1937 and 1938. Shares of Forbes's company, the Producers' and General Finance Corporation, collapsed in August 1937.[96] By November 1938, Forbes was blamed[97] for more than a quarter-of-a-million-pound loss, revealed by audits of Producers'. He resigned as managing director. He also had been advanced £36,000, which he promised to repay. He replied to attacks on his management of the company saying, "I have given almost everything, even £10,000 worth of jewels my wife had, and I am nearly ruined."[98]

Forbes was charged in court on another matter,[99] indicted with four other men "to cheat and defraud." He was still borrowing money heavily from the Scottish Loan and Finance Co., Ltd., in amounts of £12,976 and £40,475. He again promised to repay.

Forbes fled his troubles in January of 1939, a few days after throwing a big champagne party.[100] He flew to Mumbai (then called Bombay), India, but was arrested immediately on charges of conspiracy to defraud[101] in the amount of £9,450. Forbes had apparently issued himself a share certificate that he admitted was "wrongfully issued," and expressed himself "sorry." Australian authorities claimed to have a *prima facie* case and immediately sought extradition. The Indian courts heard the case and released the fugitive, amazingly, on £375 bail.

Australians later added a forgery charge so that he could be extradited from any "British" nation and France.

Not surprisingly, Forbes jumped bail again. It would not be hard, even for a foreigner, to lose himself in the underworld of Bombay, where he may

---

96 *Daily Examiner*, "Shares Collapse Producers and General Finance Corporation," August 27, 1937, page 5.
97 *Daily Advertiser*, "Shareholders' Refusal to Approve Directors' Report Sydney," November 23, 1938.
98 Ibid.
99 *Daily Advertiser*, "Conspiracy Charges Advance to John Woolcott Forbes," November 1, 1939, page 1.
100 *The Sydney Morning Herald*, "Pleads Guilty in U.S.A., Woolcott Forbes's Crimes," March 3, 1943.
101 *Singleton Argus*, "Case of John Woolcott Forbes Appeal for Extradition," January 20, 1939.

have picked up false passports. Forbes completely vanished. Sgt. Det. Nye of Sydney flew from Bombay to London and Paris and returned "completely baffled." Nye traced him to Paris, but lost him. He enlisted aid from Scotland Yard.

One paper later reported[102] that Forbes had arrived in London by airplane, where he had been traced but not arrested—despite communications between Scotland Yard and the New South Wales police.

Forbes disappears from the radar at this point, but appears to have fled to Canada. There he met Ernest Dawson, sometime between 1939 or 1940. He applied for a licence to sell securities under the name of George Blake. He was licensed as a salesman and operated in the Niagara peninsula and parts of western Ontario.[103]

Forbes moved quickly. He apparently took the initiative to work with Ernest. Ernest, in one of his letters[104] to Lynda from a New York prison, said that Forbes simply walked into his office one day. We don't know how Forbes knew that Ernest would be a compatible man to work with—there must have been word on the street. Forbes was soon working as a salesman for Ernest Dawson, according to OSC records. It's possible they continued to get to know each other at Ernest's Hunt Club, or at one of Forbes's lavish parties—or over a card game. They both loved to gamble.

Toronto was probably the perfect new home for Forbes. During the 1930s, Toronto was awash in stock speculation and there was money to be made selling dubious and non-existent mining securities.

Ernest was the perfect partner for Forbes, a respected name in the Bay Street business world, a man who had learned all the angles in the past decade, and probably a man who would be discreet about such matters as being wanted abroad. Ernest was the "front man," while Forbes (and C.W.C. Perry) worked the field.

---

102 *Recorder*, "Forbes Said to Be in London," April 1, 1939.
103 *Toronto Daily Star*, "Ontario Seeks 'Second Ponzi' Awaiting Trial in New York," January 18, 1943. It is interesting that the article did not identify the "first Ponzi," Ernest Dawson. Dawson was, after all, a respected Toronto socialite and businessman.
104 Dawson, A.E., unpublished letter from New York Federal Detention Center, November 15, 1942.

Ernest and Forbes were soon working together on Dawson's Ponzi scheme.[105] Unearned dividends were paid unsuspecting stockholders out of principal, according to the *Star*. "His manipulations centered about 'Associate Royalty Trust,' which they represented as having "vast oil holdings." The Trust was one of Ernest's shell companies, according to the OSC.

All went well for a couple of years until two investigators, Det. Sgt. James Semple and Arthur Verity, special investigator for the OSC, hit the jackpot. They were routinely checking a file of circulars on internationally wanted men. They spotted Forbes's picture, although they knew him as Blake. Investigators immediately staked out his hotel, waiting in the lobby to arrest him. They watched for a light in his room. But he did not come back to his room. The next day, investigators entered Forbes's suite but found him gone. Somehow, he'd discovered that they were on his trail. Maybe he recognized the two men in the lobby as cops.

As he did in Australia, Forbes took to the air. In his hotel room, Semple and Verity found that he had abandoned fifteen suits, three dozen shirts, six pairs of spats, a dozen pair of shoes, eight fedora hats, a top hat and cane, and tropical apparel. The wardrobe, they estimated, was worth $1,500. Although that amounts to about $25,000 in 2021 dollars, it was probably worth a lot more. Given today's eighty-dollar shirts, several-thousand-dollar tailored suits and four-hundred-dollar leather shoes, the abandoned wardrobe might now cost more than $30,000 to buy. (Besides, where would you buy spats today?)

Somewhere in his mad dash to escape the law, Forbes probably tipped off his partner, Ernest. And sometime in the following months, they met again and set up shop in New York City. Forbes bought a new wardrobe and penetrated the upper levels of New York high society. No more retired farmers and teachers. Ernest, again, was the front man, setting up the shell companies and bank accounts.

Together, Dawson and Forbes left the OSC behind to dig into the records of their fraudulent scheme, bilking Ontario investors of their hard-won cash and securities. They went to work in the lucrative field of wealthy American widows, with Forbes drawing fanciful histories for himself among the ladies, and Ernest plowing their stocks and funds into A.E. Dawson's accounts.

---

105 *Ibid.*

Warrant Charges in OSC Extradition Request

According to OSC files, the Dawson shell companies were Royalties Corporation Syndicate, Associated Royalties Trust, Management & Finance Company, Limited, and others. The OSC alleged[106] that "in only a few cases were representations made by Dawson himself." However, Ernest himself did the paperwork. He sold the stolen securities, and deposited cash or cheques in the A.E. Dawson Company bank account or with Toronto broker Rittenhouse, Hamilton & Company. He probably also wrote the phony dividend cheques from the shell companies.

Both Ernest and Perry eventually pleaded guilty to the OSC charges.

The Mabel Van Loon Operation

The Dawson-Perry-Forbes team conducted a sustained, long-term effort to acquire the stocks and savings of Mrs. Mabel Van Loon. The project provides an in-depth example of how the A.E. Dawson team worked in their Ontario operation.

According to the OSC, C.W.C. Perry and John Woolcott Forbes worked the smaller towns and rural areas of southwest Ontario. They visited Mrs. Van Loon several times over a two-year period, from mid-1940 to August 1942. First, they persuaded her to turn over a $1,000 Province of Alberta Bond, a $1,000 Dominion of Canada Bond, and $3,000 in other Dominion of Canada Bonds. Government bonds, at the time, were safe, interest-bearing securities popular with Canadians. These bonds were, ostensibly, to pay for shares or units of three shell companies.

Unknown to Mrs. Van Loon, all three new investments were shell companies recently established by A.E. Dawson. She understood that for her bonds and cash, she was buying $700 debentures in Management & Finance Company, Limited, two hundred shares of Equity Holding Corporation, and seven units of Royalties Corporation Syndicate—the shell companies.

The OSC said that Perry and Forbes told Mrs. Van Loon that Equity Holding Company stock had been in existence for many years, established

---

106 *Ibid*, page 2.

during The Great War. They assured her that it had always paid dividends and would, no doubt, continue to do so. In fact, say the court documents,[107] "the said company had been incorporated only on February 14, 1940, about a month before it was sold to Mrs. Mabel L. Van Loon, and at the time of the sale it had paid no dividends whatsoever."

Perry and Forbes had clearly identified Mrs. Van Loon as an easy mark with even greater potential. They later paid her a 7½-cent "dividend" (with help from Ernest) from "a fictitious value on certain large blocks of shares in more or less worthless mining companies representing assets of Equity Holding Corporation, Limited." (This was the first dividend ever paid by the company.)

No doubt delighted by this dividend, Mrs. Van Loon agreed to invest further, at the urgings of Perry and Forbes. They recommended the "gilt-edged security" of Management & Finance Company, Limited—which had just been incorporated by Ernest shortly before, on February 8, 1940. She also bought seven units of the Royalties Corporation Syndicate for $2,996, at a price that was purported to be "advancing rapidly." In fact, the security had no real market value "at, during, about, before, or subsequent to the time of the said sale."[108]

It was a complex scheme of interdependent fictions. Royalties Corporation Syndicate had, for instance, total assets of 6,625 shares of another shell company, the Associated Royalties Trust. Perry and Forbes assured Mrs. Van Loon that this company owned producing oil and gas leases in the United States. They would be able to resell her shares in a brief time "at a considerable profit," they declared.

Perry and Forbes subsequently returned to Mrs. Van Loon and persuaded her to further turn over three $1,000 Dominion of Canada bonds in exchange for the purchase of another shell company, Norco Thompson, preferred shares at $2.50 to $3.50 per share—which they had originally bought at twenty-five cents per share. It appears that Norco Thompson was also a shell company with no real market value. Ernest's son Ken was a director of

---

107 *Archives of Ontario file # 1250*, "Memorandum for the Attorney General's Department Re. A.E. Dawson, C.W.C. Perry, John Woolcott Forbes alias George Blake," November 13, 1942, Ontario Securities Commission, 1942, page 4.
108 *Ibid.*, page 6.

Norco Thompson, as was E.J. Thompson, Dawson's partner in several other matters. Perry and Forbes promised to return Mrs. Van Loon's bonds and a cash profit when they resold the shares.

Poor Mrs. Van Loon's head must have been spinning, at this point. There followed a series of signed contracts, forged account statements, and cash "profits." Mrs. Van Loon's real bonds somehow disappeared—the OSC alleged they were stolen. Ernest's secretary claims that her signature on an account statement was forged. The attorney general claimed that it all constituted "in view of the non-existence of any market for Norco Thompson preferred… theft by a trick." The court documents suggest that Perry and Forbes tricked not only the law and Mrs. Van Loon, but their own employer Dawson.

Summary of Charges

The individual OSC charges[109] are summarized below, with the value of cash or stolen securities (where available) indicated in 1940 dollars:

- January 1940 to June 1942: **Dawson and Forbes** re. Mrs. S.H. Blake, Toronto, Ontario, $56,727 in money, securities and shares.
- April 1940 to July 1942: **Dawson** re. Mrs. Mabel Anderson and W.H. Anderson, Wilsonville, Ontario, $2,993 in cheques, plus $500 Canada bonds, 200 shares of Teck-Hughes, 200 shares of Sylvanite, 100 shares of Walker's Preferred, 500 shares of Sullivan, and 200 shares of Sisco.
- March 1940 to April 1940: **Dawson and Forbes** re. Mrs. Mabel Anderson and W.R. Anderson, Wilsonville, Ontario, Canada Bond, $186 in cheques, $2,000 debentures of Trust and Guarantee, 30 shares of Trust and Guarantee, Buenos Aires bond, Montreal Apartments bond, 22 shares of Massey Harris, City of Brantford bond, 200 Bidwood shares.
- March 1940 to August 1940: **Dawson and Forbes** re. Mabel L. Van Loon, $1,000 Alberta bond, $4,000 Canada bonds.
- August 1940 to January 1941: **Forbes** re. Mabel Van Loon, Waterford, Ontario, forgery of Dawson signature on contract.

---

109 *Archives of Ontario, File No. 1250,* 1942, Department of Attorney General for Ontario, "Warrant in the matter of the application for Extradition of A.E. Dawson and John Woolcott Forbes, alias George Blake" to the United States of America Southern District of New York, pages 4-6.

- August 1942: **Forbes** re. Mabel Van Loon, $3,000 Canada bonds.
- June 1940: **Dawson and Forbes** re. Mary E. Johnston, St. Thomas, Ontario, $440 cheque.
- November 1941 to August 1942: **Dawson** re. Mary E. Johnston, St. Thomas, Ontario, $500 Ontario bond, $200 Canada bonds, cheque $440.
- November 1941 to June 1942: **Dawson** re. Mary E. Johnston, St. Thomas, Ontario, $553 cheques, 500 shares of Sylvanite, $600 Canada bonds, 200 shares of Aldermac.
- June 1941 to June 1942: **Dawson** re. Lila C. Knowles, St. Thomas, Ontario, $1,815 in cheques, 300 shares Sylvanite, 331 shares of San Antonia, 400 shares of Leech gold, 500 shares of Lape Cadillac, 50 shares of Imperial Oil, $4,000 Canada bonds, 500 shares of Malartic, 200 shares of Paymaster, 100 shares Hard Rock.
- June 1942 to July 1942: **Dawson** re. Lila C. Knowles, St. Thomas, Ontario, $4,000 Canada bonds.
- June 1941 to June 1942: **Dawson** re. F.M. Ward and Fred Ward, Waterford, Ontario, cheques $3,613, 70 shares of Silverwood common and preferred.
- April 1941 to June 1942: **Dawson** re. Gladys M. Nelles and Lois Nelles, Waterford, Ontario, $1,076 cash and cheques, $1,600 Canada bonds, 133 shares of Sisco, 20 shares of Hargreaves, $50 American premium, 35 shares of Moore Corporation, $1,000 Toronto bond, 300 shares of Cockshutt Plough, 10 shares of United Fruit, 15 shares of Steel of Canada, 200 shares of Macasse.
- April 1941 to June 1942: **Dawson** re. Gladys M. Nelles and Lois Nelles, Waterford, Ontario, 36 shares of Moore Corporation, 390 shares of Cockshutt Plough, $3,500 Canada bonds.
- February 1941 to June 1942: **Dawson** re. Joseph Opychany, Brantford, Ontario, $2,570 cash and cheques.
- October 1940: **Dawson and Forbes** re. Joseph Opychany, Brantford, Ontario, $979 cash and cheque.
- October 1940 to February 1941: **Dawson** re. Bertha Hodgson, 25 shares of Noranda, 200 shares of Teck-Hughes, $764 cheque.

CHAPTER 14:
The New York Operations

Only the most narcissistic of con artists (John Woolcott Forbes) would do it: choose the most prominent woman in New York City (and the wife of a well-known stockbroker) as one of his stock fraud victims. Clearly, he expected to get away with it.

A narcissistic con artist is exactly who John Woolcott Forbes appears to have been when he and Ernest Dawson moved their operations to New York City.

And only two great narcissists (both Ernest and Forbes) would ignore the SEC's huge motivation to indict a Canadian stock fraudster. *The Canadian Problem* was huge, and they chose a venue where they were the most vulnerable… on United States soil. There, American law had complete authority, and no extradition laws were necessary to pursue them.

While Forbes zeroed in on elderly, wealthy widows in the city, he also chose Mrs. Guy Percy Trulock as one of his victims. That may have been one of the biggest mistakes of his life.

Mrs. Guy Percy Trulock: An Unlikely Victim

Mrs. Trulock was Forbes' and Ernest's most famous victim. They could not have chosen a victim less likely to take fraud lying down—once she discovered the deception. She was also quite likely to discover that she was being scammed. Her husband was, after all, in the business. At the time, Mrs. Trulock was one of the most prominent and politically active women in the United States, second only, perhaps, to Eleanor Roosevelt.

She was well connected with New York and national figures. She was fiercely patriotic, and probably very angry about foreign exploitation of American investors. She was also fiercely moralistic, with a lifelong interest in promoting public and private morality.

Anyone would have predicted that Mrs. Trulock would want to expose and ruin Dawson and Forbes for their sins.

Born Musette Langford in New York City, Mrs. Trulock was educated and trained as a dramatic soprano. She married stockbroker Guy Percy Trulock and was henceforth known as "Mrs. Guy Percy Trulock." As a performer, she became the president of the Century Theater Club, a women's club. From there, in 1941, she was elected the president of the powerful and prestigious New York City Federation of Women's Clubs.

At her nomination for the post, the club's secretary endorsed her as an experienced club executive among cultural and arts groups, as well as patriotic and church organizations. "She is alive to all current civic interests of the day with an alert and courageous mind to aid in all things for the betterment of women and children and all other avenues of community service."

Mrs. Trulock had a strong interest in the United States' preparedness for war, in the years before America joined the Allies in World War II. As president of the federation, she spoke on topics such as the role of music in military, civilian, and industrial morale. She organized a meeting on the role of the consumer in defence. She was incredibly active as the voice of right-thinking American women.

In 1942, Mrs. Trulock became chairman of the New York City's Tin Can Salvage effort, a recycling program to save metal resources for the war effort and the allies. She was regularly cited and pictured in the *New York Times*. One article even describes her as riding along with neighbourhood garbage trucks to assess their metal collection efforts. She followed up this effort by recruiting 225 housewives to board sanitation trucks, to encourage the drive. By February 1943, under Mrs. Trulock's management, the city had collected more tin cans than it could process.

Just how Mrs. Trulock was bilked by the Dawson-Forbes team is unknown. We do not know how Forbes persuaded her to give up her legitimate stocks for the Dawson shell company stock. Hers was not one of the cases chosen to prosecute the two men. However, it would not be surprising if her husband, a prominent stockbroker, was chagrined to discovered that she was exchanging valuable, legitimate stock for the worthless shell company stock that Forbes was selling. And once it was discovered, it would not be surprising that Forbes and Dawson may have found themselves at the mercy of the eminent, passionate, and well-connected woman.

Mrs. Trulock's case was not actually used in the formal indictment. Perhaps she did not have adequate documentation of the scheme. However, she apparently had no problem with her name appearing in numerous newspaper stories about the fraud. Almost every major story about the scheme listed her as a prominent victim.

Hell hath no fury...

After the war, in 1954, Mrs. Trulock became even more famous. In the wake of McCarthyism, she took on the position of administrator for the notorious Code Authority of the Comics Magazine Association of America. She was essentially the censor for the huge comic book industry in the United States. This crusading organization strove to eliminate "sordid and objectionable" material from the hugely popular, comic-publishing industry, which sold hundreds of millions of comic books every year. Under Mrs. Trulock, comic books had to be reviewed before publication, and were published only when they could display her "Approved by the Comics Code Authority" stamp on the cover page. *MAD* magazine escaped her purview only by changing from a comic book to a magazine format. Mrs. Trulock administered the controversial censor organization until 1965.

The indefatigable Mrs. Trulock died in the Midwest on August 8, 1972, outliving Ernest Dawson, who had bilked her in 1941, by four years.

Forbes Takes the Lead

John Woolcott Forbes clearly ran from Ontario and decamped to New York in a big hurry. It is not clear, however, how long Ernest took to transfer his efforts there. He probably operated out of both locations for a while, and finally abandoned Ontario when he realized that OSC inquiries had begun.

Ernest's letters—and notes in the *Toronto Star* society pages—indicate that he had conducted U.S. business from the posh Biltmore Hotel for some time. (He also wrote with familiarity about the hotel in the novel he wrote years later.) Until 1940, he may have been conducting conventional, more or less legitimate securities business there.

Forbes, however, took the opportunity to infiltrate the high society organizations.[110] The move to New York City marked a change in *modus operandi* for the team, not just a change in geography. Forbes had moved comfortably in Australia's high society. He may have suggested to Ernest, why not elevate their operations from rural pensioners to more wealthy investors? There was more money to be made there, while the same human foibles—gullibility and greed—motivated wealthy people as much as retired farmers. Thus the Dawson-Forbes team focused on a new target group: the wealthy citizens of New York City.

Working from his room in the Biltmore, Ernest again served the operation as the financial, behind-the-scenes front man, while Forbes snagged and seduced the victims in person. Purporting to act as Forbes's broker, Ernest wrote the correspondence, mailed the stock certificates, endorsed the stock certificates and cheques, wrote cheques for phony dividends, sold stock obtained from the victims, and deposited their money into the A.E. Dawson & Company accounts. In actual fact, say the indictments, A.E. Dawson & Company was not acting as a broker in the purchase and sale of securities for the victims. In fact, he was acting as a principal and deposited the earnings in his own name (or sometimes using the front Edie Millward and Company to cover up his personal interests in the matter).

Meanwhile, Forbes managed to obtain a membership in the prestigious Advertising Club of New York. The club was awash with wealthy advertising executives and their wives. The membership included many vulnerable, elderly women who were susceptible to Forbes's considerable charms—and promises of even more money.

Legal documents mention Forbes's string of U.S. aliases, including "John Hamilton," "John Warburg Hamilton," "Reginald G.A. Forbes," "George De Pledge," "George Watson," and Ontario's "George Blake." In the Advertising

---

110 Many of the facts in this chapter arise from two hundred pages of legal documents in the United States National Archives, under the names of A.E. Dawson, John Woolcott Forbes, and C.W.C. Perry. The documents describe the arrests and transport of the men from Mexico City to Texas, and the specific grand jury charges laid against them at that time, in October 1942.

Club, he used the name John Hamilton most often. He had a collection of stories to go with each name, carefully tailored to suit the intended victim.

SEC Frustrations

Meanwhile, the SEC had been trying for years to prosecute Canadian securities fraudsters for their U.S. activities. Their attempts had failed largely because the frauds mostly took place in Ontario. Canadian, Ontario, and U.S. officials could not work together successfully. In particular, a Canadian using the U.S. mail for fraud was not a crime in Canada, and therefore such criminals would not be extradited at U.S. request.

The Lund report outlines the SEC's decades of frustrations with prosecuting Canadian swindlers. Beginning in the mid-1930s, they struggled with:
- no Canadian federal stock fraud laws,
- the non-cooperation and outright hostility of the Ontario securities commissioner,
- the lack of a functioning extradition treaty to handle securities fraud, and
- the general attitude in Canada that the U.S. should just leave Bay Street securities men and the Canadian mining industry alone.

Ernest *et al.* decided to work U.S. investors out of New York City, instead of from Bay Street, where most of the other Canadian fraudsters originated. Ernest was *physically present* on U.S. soil in New York, and he used the U.S. mail for many of his transactions. This directly violated U.S. law and made him subject to U.S. mail fraud, forgery, and registration laws. He and Forbes could be arrested on U.S. soil for violations of U.S. law. No extradition or Canadian cooperation was necessary to prosecute.

By camping at the Biltmore and posting correspondence in a red U.S. mailbox, Ernest set up his operation for eventual capture and prosecution by the SEC.

Ernest's operation had an identifiable, targeted group of victims—starting with the wealthy widows of the Advertising Club of New York. He used the United States mail for much of his communications. Acting on some kind of tip or complaint, the SEC began tracing correspondence between A.E. Dawson & Company and members of the club. It is likely that some of the victims were not club members—like Mrs. Guy Percy Trulock, for instance—but people to whom Forbes obtained introductions through other connections.

The Advertising Club of New York[111] was founded in 1896 as an elite group of advertising professionals who met to discuss the marketing business. It began as the Sphinx Club and then became the Advertising Club in 1915. By 1927, the group had become a prestigious organization. It hosted U.S. presidents, New York mayors, princes, and international dignitaries. The club established uniform professional standards in advertising and gave rise to today's Better Business Bureau. By the 1940s, it had become a high-powered group of men and women with a lot of money to invest.

Forbes: A Master at Conning the Upper Class

With Ernest conducting the financial infrastructure of the operation, Forbes went to work among the Advertising Club's membership, posing as a wealthy, romantic figure. He obtained introductions to large numbers of female friends and acquaintances.

Assistant U.S. Attorney Edward J. Behrens later described Forbes's operations to the press. He said the man was "almost fantastic" and was wanted in half a dozen states and Canada.

The SEC court documents say that he told the New York ladies an assortment of intriguing tales about himself, in what sounds like a charm offensive designed to fascinate, reassure, and attract elderly women. The SEC documents outline his claims, including that:

- he was a Secret Service agent of the British government (how exciting!),
- he was a financial expert on foreign exchange (very reassuring),
- he had written a book on foreign exchange (most credible),
- he was a bachelor and a man of great wealth (very attractive),
- he was investing money for friends and acquaintances of the victims (reassuring, again),
- his associate Edward W. Vardin of Rochester, New York, was a vice president of Bethlehem Steel Corporation (impressive),

---

111   https://www.theadvertisingclub.org/finder/1/history, June 2021.

- he was a member of the British Purchasing Commission (big money here), and
- that he was a business associate of Charles Dawes, former vice president of the United States under President Calvin Coolidge (impressive, again).

This astounding list of stories illustrates Forbes's intense degree of Machiavellian manipulation—and the high degree of psychopathy involved. One can only imagine that he must have conducted these deceptions without a shred of empathy. Each of the claims was entirely false, said the government. He was, in fact, still married to his Australian wife.

Forbes used the claims to persuade the women—and some men—to "part with their money and property" by purchasing shares, units, and debentures of the various mining and shell companies created by Ernest. Forbes went to such lengths as to arrange letters from him to the victims to be mailed from various places, to mislead them concerning his whereabouts. He even proposed marriage to some of the ladies.

As in Ontario, Ernest guaranteed the signatures of victims on their marketable stock certificates so that he could sell them and obtain the proceeds. These guarantees were the basis for later forgery charges, which were eventually dropped.

At some point, the Dawson-Forbes-Perry team must have realized that they were under investigation. Some of their victims had carefully preserved their correspondence, which became evidence for mail fraud, and the basis for many U.S. indictments.

And happily for the U.S. authorities, the Dawson team had committed their crimes on U.S. soil. There was no need for futile negotiations with Canadian authorities, and no need for extradition.

Ernest and Forbes disappeared from New York into Mexico. In Mexico City, Ernest had an office, a secretary, and a lawyer. He apparently had been exploring legitimate investment opportunities there, including forest lands.

The U.S. Indictments

Federal attorneys in the Southern District of New York presented their evidence against Ernest and Forbes to a grand jury. The case was based on technical evidence—dated envelopes and correspondence—and involved just a fraction of the victims actually affected. However, the evidence held up in court, and both men pleaded guilty. It was one of the first successful prosecutions against *The Canadian Problem*. The case was widely covered in the *New York Times* and back home in the Toronto press.

I travelled to New York City to examine the archived materials of the indictments, almost two hundred pages of legal documents. Once again, I was struck by the fact that real crimes were involved, with real victims. Ernest's attorneys could not deny the carefully gathered evidence against their client.

Ernest and Forbes were both charged with selling shares or units "by false and fraudulent pretenses, practices, representations and promises, and by false and fraudulent artifices and devices to part with their money and property"[112] of Chappie-Mammoth Gold Mines, Associate Royalty Trust, Royalties Corporation Syndicate, and Management & Finance Company, Limited. The mines and corporations were listed as co-defendants in the indictments, their shares and units essentially worthless, despite their conservative, solid-sounding names. The companies involved were all headquartered in Toronto.

While only ten victims were listed in the U.S. indictment, "diverse other persons" affected were not listed. This was because of their great number and the lack of indictable information available to the grand jury regarding their cases. The counts actually used in the indictments mostly concerned mail fraud, with dated, stamped envelopes as the chief evidence, the defendants having used the U.S. mail and "knowingly devised and intended to devise a scheme and artifice to defraud." In a separate count, the two men were accused of forging a signature on the back of a U.S. Treasury cheque made out to Mrs. Mary Jane Frey. This charge was the count later used to justify the arrest in Mexico and their transfer to Texas for arrest.

---

112 Indictment, U.S. District Court, United States of America *vs* John Woolcott Forbes with aliases, Alfred Ernest Dawson with alias, Canadian Management Company, Inc., Management and Finance Co., Limited, and Chappie-Mammoth Gold Mines, Limited. December 4, 1942. U.S. National Archives.

The ten victims officially listed as fraud victims were: Monroe Bickart, Mary Jane Frey, Sam Goldberg, Matilda Kranichfeld, Nan Malkind, Minnye W. Nolan, Christina W. Ross, Robert Ross, Helen W. Smith, and George R. Stele. Many were wealthy widows, and one was an elderly woman living in a nursing home.

The shell stock were offered, probably in person by Forbes, by telephone calls, and by mail, and in telegrams originated by Ernest. The Dawson team claimed to their victims that there was a *bona fide* market for the Canadian securities, valued at hundreds of dollars per unit. Also, they claimed that the securities were sound, dividend-paying units with hundreds of thousands of dollars in assets behind them. None of this was true.

The victims were told that Chappie-Mammoth shares were valued at twenty-five cents per share, whereas Dawson had paid only 1½ cents per share. The charges also involved the Canadian Management Company, a corporation organized by Dawson under the State of Oklahoma. The company was, according to the charges, "dominated by and under to conceal Alfred Ernest Dawson's true interest in the transaction." Canadian Management Company supposedly had oil and gas interests with income to Associate Royalty Trust and Royalties Corporation Syndicate. It was a complicated, sophisticated scheme.

The victims were sometimes paid "dividends" for their investments. According to the charges, the "dividends" paid to the victims had no relationship to either the total number of units outstanding, or to the number of units owned by each victim. Dividend cheques were mailed from a phony address on Wall Street. This was the "Ponzi" part of the scheme, and also Ernest's task to engineer and carry out.

CHAPTER 15:
The Mexican Adventure: Part 1

This chapter, and the next, include Ernest's written masterpiece, his account of being arrested, jailed, and kidnapped in Mexico City. The story is a great adventure, the tale of an upper-middle-class white man encountering the criminal justice system for the first time—in a foreign land.

This story made me love my grandfather again, despite all his crimes and misdemeanours, despite the whole tawdry history of fraud and white-collar crime. How could I resist this incredible memoir, with its colourful detail and wry humour? How could I resist the earthy honesty of the story?

While Ernest and Forbes transferred their activities to Mexico, the U.S. authorities in the Southern District of New York compiled indictments against the two in a grand jury process. Once the indictments were written, they could arrest the two men. The problem was that Dawson and Forbes had got their wind up in New York and had apparently fled. An international manhunt ensued, but the two were finally located in Mexico City in October of 1942.

However, for the New York indictments, the two men had to be arrested on United States soil in order to be prosecuted under U.S. law. So, how did they get to the U.S.? This is the story of how it happened.[113]

This long, colourful account,[114] written by Ernest himself, was probably composed just months later in the West Street, New York, federal detention centre and typed up subsequently. He may have submitted it to U.S. authorities as part of his claim of illegal arrest and transport.

In some ways this account is the very heart of Ernest's story. It is the ten pivotal days that were the turning point of his life, from being a respected securities dealer, to being sought and treated as a common criminal.

Ernest's story reads like a piece of fiction. One moment he is walking down the street in Mexico City and the next moment he finds himself in a squalid, surreal, concrete cell.

My father, Donald Dawson, noted on the file in the wooden trunk: "This is an account of dad's stay in a Mexican jail for some 7-10 days + or -. Written with a stubbie pencil. Amazed that these boxes were left with him to be later transcribed into ink and then typewritten out (not exact copy)."

Ernest's account describes an "adventure" and does not address the charges against himself and Forbes. Indeed, the story is written from the point of view of an innocent but unfortunate man.

---

113 Two accounts exist of A.E. Dawson and John Woolcott Forbes's arrests in Mexico City and their "extradition" to the United States. The first is a deposition by Forbes's attorney George F. Reid. In dry legalese, Reid describes the two men's arrest and transport to Texas. The deposition was created to support Woolcott's claim that the men had been illegally detained and transported to the U.S. for arrest. That claim did not affect their legal outcomes.

The second account, Ernest Dawson's own, agrees with the Reid document in most particulars This document is included in this chapter. The typewritten version is slightly different from the handwritten version. For the most part, the long, original, handwritten version is transcribed here, with Ernest's original spelling and grammar. Some additions from the typewritten version have been added.

114 Dawson, A.E., Prison Notes, unpublished, circa 1943.

South of the Border: Down Mexico Way South
By A.E. Dawson

My arrest took place in Mexico. I had not turned fifty-five years of age and had completed over thirty-five years of business connected with a more or less conscious rectitude. I have never been able to determine why Mexico should have been chosen for this event. My business affairs were centered in Toronto, New York, Los Angeles, and Mexico City. And I was in the habit of making the second of these by air every few weeks. Any of these periods other than Mexico City would have been more practical and from my point of view, clearly preferable.

Mexican newspapers, as I well know, were persuaded with little concern as to their many inaccuracies, and even less regard for the libel laws, but I had never thought of these matters having any possible personal consideration. However, some months after my arrest, my secretary, with an amused expression on her face, handed me an old Mexico City daily and pointed to a photograph of myself which appeared on the front page. It was captioned by the Spanish equivalent of "Two-Gun Man" and an accompanying article ran a brief account of my arrest, referring to a report that I was wanted by the police of several countries as an international crook with a record of countless scamming into millions of dollars, and concluded with the statement that I never went about on the street without a brace of pistols stuck in my belt.

I recognized the article for what it was, a journalistic presentation inspired by the U.S. officials who "engineered" my arrest, in order to give substance to their tutelary demands upon the Mexican police, for their cooperation, and a shadow of justification for their part in my subsequent abduction. So far as I have been able to discover, the Toronto newspapers missed this bit of artistic journalism. The "Two-gun" reference at least would have impressed my deer-hunting and skeet-shooting companions of Bay Street who always had a dim view of my qualities of marksmanship.

The arrest occurred in the lobby of the Ritz Hotel, and one of the officers was a U.S. Customs man acting for the U.S. Secret Services, the other an official of the Mexican police. We went out on the busy street and had gone only a few yards when I was crowded into a store entrance and quickly and expertly frisked for guns. Finding nothing of the sort, we continued to the office of the Chief of Police of the city.

My introduction to this person was a highly formal one and he shook hands with me. I returned his verbal greetings in my limited Spanish and felt the situation to be rather incongruous, in several of its aspects. A conversation ensued in rapid Spanish which I was unable to follow, and I did fancy that I observed some reluctance on the part of the chief to participate in an illegal action against a national of another country and one against whom Mexico had no complaint.

After a time I was taken to in an anteroom where a number of clerks were at work. Thinking to telephone a lawyer I had had occasion to employ a few times, I reached for a nearby telephone but instantly the clerks sounded a chorus of protests and I was made to sit on the other side of the room well out of reach of the instrument. Eventually I was taken to a prison some distance away but within the city limits and the two officers left me saying they would return in an hour.

I had made repeated requests to be permitted to contact my lawyer but each time had been put off with an evasive reply. Here I demanded that the British Consul be informed of my arrest but met with a decided negative. I was registered as to my name only and my pockets emptied. Some three pesos in silver, a pocket-sized Spanish-English dictionary, a stick of pencil, and my pipe and nearly empty tobacco pouch were returned to me. Through a courtyard flavored with a brilliant sun of a Mexican afternoon, I was led to a solitary cell where a heavy steel door stood open and two women and several children were ejected with their scarce belongings to make way for me. In the fashion of such places these people had been given the use of the cell in which they could live while their men-folk were serving brief sentences. Their belongings comprised only a charcoal brazier upon which they cooked food for themselves and their prisoner husbands, a blanket apiece and a few cooking utensils. I entered upon my occupation of their quickly excavated quarters and the solid door clanged behind me. The snap of the heavy padlock sounded like a clang of doom.

The hour was 3:25 PM. Thursday, October 15th, 1942.

I took stock of my cell. It was about five feet wide, ten feet long, and perhaps fifteen feet high. Air and light entered through a circular opening high up in the wall and an electric light was burning close to the ceiling. The walls were solid and... the floor cement and the furnishings absolutely nil, except for a toilet, a seat without a seat. A litter of newspapers lay in a scattered pile on the floor and in one corner was an entire brick—evidently the base for the charcoal braziers. One thing there was known to soften the hard mass of the place and, transitory as it was, I rejoiced in it. Down in one corner a small, lighted candle such as are used by Mexican peons everywhere to celebrate their numerous saints' days. I regarded it as a good omen; the sight of it comforted me and I uttered silently a prayer to whatever saint might be referenced in this particular instance. The candle flickered in an hour or so, then quietly died.

Contemplating my cell, the cement floor then was to be my bed, the brick my pillow; the newspapers lying about would have to serve for mattress and for covering.

In the steel door I discovered two small bolt holes through which I was able to see something of what went on in the courtyard and I occupied myself in this until my disturbed entrance settled a little, after which I set about doing what I could to clean up my quarters.

My experience with Mexico's pestiferous "mañana" had warned me against a too literal interpretation of the officer's promise to return in one hour. Several days later I was still waiting their return; as the afternoon wore on I became more and more accustomed to the strange sights in the courtyard, visible through my small peephole. There was a milling about of men, women, and children. Because of the lack of uniforms it was not possible for me always to identify prison officials or employers. For the most part the men in the yard were loafing in the sun; the women were washing clothes or fussing over their cooking pots, forever engaged in some task or another.

The courtyard had a gentle slope down to a drain in the center and one young man seemed to be always engaged in pushing, poking, and washing the litter of the place down the drain in the center. I saw amazing piles of rubbish disappear with the aid of the hose pipe. My interest was technical in nature. It was incomprehensible to me how what appeared to be an ordinary sized drain pipe could be so accommodating.

After which I began to wonder if any provision was made by which prisoners were fed. It was obvious that those who had women folk in the courtyard would be taken care of—and that probably a communal effort in this was in effect. And there seemed no answer to my individual problem, unattended as I was. Eventually the door opened and a three ounce roll of bread was thrust in, and once more the door closed upon me. I was very apprehensive at first about the light, but it never failed me. Night and day it continued to burn and I was spared the long night of darkness which might have been the first night. I settled my head on the brick, kicked off my shoes and settled down on these floor sheets of newspapers. Had my floor been as well covered as my brick and my body protected as my head was from the too-solid cement, it would not have been as bad.

Late in the morning came my regulation bread roll. And again late in the afternoon. Late in the evening came the third and final meal of the day. There was a slight change in the menu. It was a 3 oz.

roll of bread but when I went down to pick it from the doorstep I was met by the baleful and unwinking eye of a fish that had been placed lengthwise in the roll, its head sticking out. Examining it more closely I found it to be a whole fish. I mean whole, and its glassy eyes told me of what I might, and did, find inside. It tasted pretty good however, by this time I was becoming less and less fastidious. It did remind me however that I had nothing to drink since arriving in this place and I commenced to conjure up a night of agony from thirst. Hearing later, it must have been midnight, a step in the courtyard I kicked the door making as much noise as I could. Surprisingly enough the door was opened and I darted out passed the turnkey and over to a tap which I had seen in operation during the day. Alas I had forgotten stories I had heard that most of the water tap in Mexico was out off before midnight And I crept back in my cell with grave fear of the night. I could have asked for a drink but I had learned to drink no water or milk or other cooked or boiled liquids of whose origin I had no knowledge. This is probable also that my request would have met with no response.

As it happened I was able to dismiss the matter from mind and the night passed off much as had the previous one.

Speaking in painful English, a boy's soft voice came to me through the edge of the doorway. "Mister you want anything?" I responded eagerly, "Si, si, cigarros." The voice replied, "One peso, please." Mindful of my limited finances I cautiously asked, "How many cigarros?" The answer came back, "Two packs." I slid a silver peso under the door, one-third of my immediate capital. Somehow I had faith in that voice. My tobacco had run out and I was badly in need of a smoke, among many other things. In a short time the boy pushed two packs of Monte Carlos and a small packet of matches under the door. For a confirmed pipe smoker they were poor things, but welcome and I consciously did not begrudge the boy his 30% profit.

I was able that morning to obtain a drink and alas for the first time, a wash. It was just a splash about the head and neck. There was no soap but I felt the better for it nevertheless.

The boy came again later with his soft, low voice. "Mister you want anything?" This time I asked for a morning paper thinking I might find it something which would throw some light upon my arrest. The boy asked again for ten centavos which I thrust out to him, wondering how he could make a profit on that. The answer to my query came with the paper. It was the third section of a three-day old paper… picked up anywhere and completely useless to me except as an addition to my bedding. I had no interest in the doings of Mexico City social set, another that this and a few advertisements it contained nothing. I was glad having about my contact with the boy; it had some hopeful possibilities. For by this time I was getting very hungry. I still had hopes of the promised return of the officials but steeled myself for this waiting.

Hearing the boy's voice outside I signalled to him and he came quickly. I tried to make him understand that I wanted to get a message to the British Consul, but that was beyond our common effort. Tearing a piece of white paper from an advertisement I wrote out in careful dictionary Spanish a summary of my wishes. It had three headings:

<u>No. 1:</u> I wanted a meal. I had money in the prison office which could be used to pay for same.

<u>No. 2:</u> I wanted my lawyer to come to see me. I appended his telephone number and name.

<u>Number 3:</u> I asked for the British Consul to be informed of my arrest, if no. 2 was not permissible and I slid the message to the waiting boy.

Through a peephole I watched him take the message to a group of men loafing in the yard. They each had a hearty laugh and I did not share this mirth. The boy came back to the door and said, "Un momento, mister." And went off. Sometime later as I was looking out I saw a clerk come into the yard and the boy take him my message. I tried to find some comfort from the expression on his face, but there was none. I stuck to the boy and the boy went off again to the office. In a little while a turnkey came and asked me if I wanted to eat! This was the third day! As casually as I could I said, "Yes," and added that there was money in the office he could use for the purpose. With the help of my Spanish-English dictionary and the cooperation of a small crowd of bystanders I made him understand that my money had been taken from me and that he should obtain what he needed for a meal, from that source... he went off and that rather definitely seemed to be the end of that.

I had another visit from the boy. "You want anything Mister?" In spite of my depressed mood, I could not help laughing. In the sickest relations of words and in the best of the King's English at my command I informed him that a statement of my wants at that moment would fill two columns of Mexico City's biggest newspaper but it was of course wasted effort, and I felt some relief. I then carefully and painstakingly waited this previous formula, i.e. a meal, my lawyer, and for the British Consul. The boy returned in a few minutes and explained through this crack, "eat is impossible," and afterwards I ignored the matter entirely.

I had by this time written so many notes that I could imagine myself in Munich, and the date 1938. I sensed the fact that I had acquired a fame equal to that of the Munich noteworthies since each time the door opened the entire group of courtyard lawyers would crowd around. Once I turned on them angrily and told them all to go to the devil. They did not understand the words and may have sensed my annoyance. At all events they laughed louder than ever. This outburst of temper did me good and I calmed down quickly afterwards, and even felt a bit ashamed. I had a feeling then that they were after all not laughing at me but with me.

With the bit of stub of a lead pencil left with me I have scribbled in large printed letters on the arch above my door, the words: "My mind to me a kingdom Is" and every now and again I would look at it and make myself believe it.

Some reporters and camera-men came to interview some bandits in the cell next to mine. While waiting about one of them picked up the hose which lay on the ground and played the water about the yard. As I watched him from my peephole I saw him take deliberate aim at the small aperture at the bottom of my door. He flooded my floor and spoiled a good deal of paper bedding before I was able by hammering on the door and yelling at him to get him to stop. There seemed little prospect that I should find a dry spot in which to lie this coming night.

Early in the morning there had been presented at my door, a strange figure... After a very official rattling of the padlock, the door opened wide and both turnkeys stood before me. Between them stood a slight erect figure clad from head to heels in a black cape and wearing a broad-brimmed hat of the shape of a priest of the Inquisition except that priests of any category were not at this time sanctioned in Mexico in their garb out of doors at least. I was instantly reminded, with some sinking of feeling, of the infamous execution of Louis XIV Monsieur Paris. He stood there completely still and completely silent, regarding me with a thoroughly completely comprehensive stare. I was so surprised at his sudden and unexpected appearance, so taken aback at the picture he made at my doorway, his dark complexion, his perfectly curled mustache, and his distracted and impersonal scrutiny, that before I had a chance to come to my senses the door had clanged to and without a single word, he had gone. I kicked myself for a stupid ass, he probably had been my chance to request a contact with the British Consul or my lawyer and I had missed it.

In mid-afternoon, it was Saturday; I was conducted to the office and into the presence of the officers who had arrested me. Regrets were offered at "unavoidable delays, etc." Then "Would you waive extradition to the U.S.?" I would. "Could you pay your own fare to the U.S. and would you?" I could and would. Very good, he went at once and arranged it at the Police Chief's office for immediate departure. One of the officers pulled out a pass and handed it to a bystander to get some coffee and cakes for me. Smilingly disregarding my repeated requests for a lawyer, etc., it was indicated that the interview was over and I was taken back to my cell. I felt much better and promised myself that in an hour or two at most I would be on my way to the U.S. for whatever purpose I cared not. Any change would be a change for the better and I went back into isolation with a light heart.

In due course the coffee and cakes came. The coffee was in a whiskey bottle and it was cold but sweet and I enjoyed it. I now had something in which to keep water in my cell.

The remainder of the Saturday passed, then Sunday, with no further word. On Monday morning I consoled myself with the thought that "all things pass away"—I thought "This too shall pass." I would by now pull at my beard and my shirt would stand on its tail. As for my person I cannot even now bear to think of it. My teeth tasted like coals.

What a Sunday it had been! One scene saved from my peephole should be recorded. It was obvious that all the women in the court yard were poverty-stricken. Most of them had but two garments and these so ragged as they scarcely afforded any protection. One of them I had never seen appeared in a nightgown and she, poor soul, had but one. Most of them were barefooted. Such garments as they had, they endeavored to keep clean by scrubbing and in turns the bright sun quickly drying them on the branches of the courtyard. The boss was eternally playing on clothes lying on the concrete the water being directed on the garment whilst the women scrubbed it.

On Sunday it appeared these persons as well as their clothes came in for a hosing. One rather tragic looking soul took off her outer dress and with only her inner garments on submitted to a hosing at the hands of some of the numerous loafers. Her slip would not stay on however and eventually she gave up all attempts at keeping herself covered, partially covered herself and observed her entirely nude being scrubbed with soap by some woman and two men, a policeman in uniform playing the hose on her. She got a cleansing from head to toe which made me almost envy her There was much laughter among the crowd of onlookers but it seemed to have no offense in it. The woman had about her a gravity and a beauty of countenance that defied loss of dignity. Naked as she was and surrounded by laughing nitwits her bearing lifted her above it all, better than a model 1900 bathing suit could have done. She appeared to be about forty and when the operation was completed someone loaned her a long strip of cloth which she hung about her shoulders, its folds hanging down in front and she sat on a bench while her clothes dried. Within an hour I saw her dressed again, her thick black hair done nicely in place, and a small white flower over one ear. She had deep, steady dark eyes, quite a handsome countenance, an even in her rags looked every bit as much a lady as any colonial lady.

In the evening I had been able for the sum of 50 centavos to get a cooking pot of coffee and two small cakes. The coffee was cold but again it was well sweetened and consisted of mostly milk. I thought to heat it and placed the cooking pot on the brick which I had been using as a pillow and left a margin of the pot reach out over the edge. For first I used twisted bits of paper and soon had it quite hot. In doing so however I had taken no thought of what would become of the smoke. I discovered that the wind would not let it out of the rose-like opening up above me and for a little while I feared I would be choked to death by the smoke which filled the room. It cleared however and the coffee was still hot when I had recovered sufficiently to try it.

If my smoke had escaped through the small cracks in the door no one appeared to have noticed it. Prison life I discovered was without past or future: it had only a present.

I had frequently heard the term "local jail" without paying it any thought. Now it reminded me of Stephen Leacock's remark about "new beer" during prohibition. "Who ever," he said, "called it new beer" was a damned poor judge of distance. To this we note of jail the adjective "local" is quite meaningless and without significance. It is just jail. It is his whole cosmos, I tried to console myself with the thought that I had had over fifty-five years of freedom, plenty, I told myself, for any one man. "Now," I said to myself, "here is your chance to rise above self, to sink into contemplation, to float along on an even keel, etc., etc." I found however that I wanted to do some of those things. I did not want either to rise or sink or float. I wanted to get out.

Many penal reforms occurred at that time, the principal one being the complete abolition of prisons. I felt sure it was a brilliant idea. This I thought: "It's the compulsory future that sticks out in all prison sentences. Remove that and priests and one would have all prison reform necessary."

I found my melancholy getting the better of me at times. It became necessary to avoid moralizing and return to reality. In one of his interminable introductions Scott remembers that a story "must be probable." One could not write about what event on at place and remain within that qualification. An instance might be given. At some point shortly after midnight of the fourth day the quiet was suddenly shortened by a fight begun by two women in the yard behind my cell, the noise of it coming in through the rose opening, over my head. More spontaneous than my dog in wolf-fight there could not possibly be anything else quite like it. I pray whatever gods may be that I never meet the woman with the hyena-like snap and snarl in her shrill tones. The fight commenced on the shrillest of top notes of which the human voice is capable and lasted for a period of perhaps ten minutes with fury describable only by a Dante or a Milton.

It ended as suddenly as it began and the silence was ominous as death. The night was startling in the depth of its quiet.

In the morning of the fifth day, it was Monday. I looked out of my peephole to find the policeman of the day before washing his socks. He had removed his cavalry boots.

Surprisingly Monday was not just another day. In the continuous bedlam that was the courtyard I heard an English speaking voice. The source of it was close by my door and I called to him. I found he was a new arrival with some experience of the operations of the prison and I explained something of my position in the hope of learning what was transpiring. He left me saying he would make some quick enquiries and a little later I saw him sitting on a bench beside a young woman who was eating oranges. Then I saw her leave him and in a moment or two an orange came sailing in my rose-hole as I had by this time come to regard it because of this petal-like bars around the aperture.

It was a life saver as in five days I had barely enough to eat to keep me on my feet and the man with the rolls had passed me by entirely that day. Never before had I and probably never again shall I have an orange equal that one. I invoked blessings on the little woman which I hope was duly received.

In a short time my English speaking friend returned to tell me he had learned a little of my affairs. There appeared to be some doubt about what action should be taken with me but until that doubt was cleared away it was decided I should remain where I was. The only comfort that provided was the assurance that I had not been completely forgotten. I then enlisted the aid of this man in an effort to get some food, asking him to make representations to someone in authority to permit me to use some of my own funds for the purpose. It worked, and two or three hours later my door opened: a fried half chicken, a fresh roll of bread, some cakes, and coffee were thrust in to me. The news of it must have reached the bread man for he never appeared again during the remainder of my stay. The next morning I put the chicken bones in the cooking pot and poured water over them from my whiskey bottle, and with wisps of paper the rest made some soup. Before the meal arrived I had developed a racking chest cough from the cold floor and it had kept me from sleeping; but after the meal this disappeared and I had a good night's sleep.

In retiring I had emulated the habits of a dog, in that I gradually lowered myself to the ground turning around and around as I did, so in an effort to find the best place among the few papers for my poor bones to rest. I had been sadly in need of something to read and I had the several sheets of old newspapers, but it was poor entertainment at last. Also I had exhausted my cigarettes and tobacco. Following this I had been saving butts and these together with some I had found belonging to former inhabitants I managed an extra couple of pipefuls.

I found there was some logic in deception. Had I imagined at the outset that I should have been left there for all those days it would have been scarcely supportable. I had determinedly kept my mind from thoughts of my family and their concerns as my whereabouts. Only by doing so could I face up. I found it curious that those who had been always the ever-present centre of my affections, hopes and desires should now become the source of my greatest mental agony.

One after another two wild looking Mexican youths climbed up to the opening in the wall, one climbing upon the shoulders of the other, and each in turn looked down at me inquiringly. I had nothing to give them and presently they left me alone.

Without warning of any kind, on the seventh day, my door was suddenly opened and I was taken to the office, wearing a week's beard, my clothes in a frightful condition, and none too vigorous in mind or body. In the office I found my secretary and my Mexico City lawyer—with them was another lawyer. I must have presented a curious sight to their eyes but to my eyes they looked angelic, something from a better world.

I learned that ever since the day of my disappearance my lawyer and my secretary had been searching for me. Failing to locate me the lawyer had enlisted the aid of the other lawyer who was closer to the councils of the powers that be in Mexico and had finally discovered my whereabouts and had secured permission to come and see me. In the meantime my family in Toronto had been contacted by telephone and my lawyer there had been advised of my disappearance and was awaiting news resulting from the search. There was nothing he could do about it since a good lawyer was on the job in Mexico City.

I was given assurance that arrangements would be made to remove me to a more civilized place of detention the next morning, and I returned to my cell with renewed hope.

CHAPTER 16:
Kidnapped to Texas: Mexican Adventure Part 2

Ernest continued his account of his Mexican adventure. He picks up after being transferred from the first jail. Like all good stories, we feel relief as he's brought back to civilization from the Mexican jail. Surely things will get back on track!

> It was a sort of a political house of detention to which I was taken and there I was able to bathe, shave, and change my linens, a suitcase full of my requirements having been brought by my secretary. Later in the day the two lawyers came to see me again and with them I was taken to see the Chief of the Police of the Republic. Here my property was returned to me, less a hundred peso note and some twenty odd dollars of U.S. money. I mentioned to remark upon this subtraction from my funds. The police chief looked up at his assistant who was standing at his side, looked back at me, and shrugged his shoulders.
>
> I looked at the chief, shrugged my shoulders, and signed the receipt.
>
> At this interview the Chief was informed by the lawyers that an appointment had been made for eleven o'clock the next morning with the Secretary of State for a discussion of my situation—and could they have the Chief's assurance that no action of any kind would be taken by the Chief in my case until after this eleven

o'clock meeting mentioned. The Chief gave his assurance on this point and I returned to my new quarters and sat down to the first respectable meal in more than a week. It had been sent in time and I had paid the wife of the governor of this house to prepare it for me. I was relaxing in a feeling of unwanted cleanliness and had gone two thirds through the mail when I was informed that I was wanted immediately. I left everything as it was and went as directed down to the front door. Here I was quietly but firmly led into a huge station wagon such as might be used by a prosperous firm. The words "Republic of Mexico" had been painted on the sides in a large circle and the engine was running.

I guessed what was up but was of course powerless to do anything about it. An armed Mexican policeman was at the wheel, and two others, one on each side of me, took the second seat. Two American officers of the U.S. Secret Service sat behind me in the third seat. Like a sheep being led to the slaughter, I was trapped and we set off at once at a rapid pace for what I rightly guessed to be the U.S. border, some 750 miles to the north.

All my personal belongings, including my all-important passport, were left behind in my quarters and my request to be permitted to pick them up was denied.

By the time we were free of the city it had become a night of brilliant moonlight. Once again I had disappeared from kin. I decided there was nothing to be done except make the best of it and I gradually became intrigued by the somewhat dramatic quality and setting of my abduction. We were traveling at a high rate of speed along the sides of the rugged mountains, thousands of feet above us on one side and thousands of sheer drop on the other, with peaks of numerous other mountains clearly visible in the brilliant moonlight. It was a light fit for a ride of the Valkyries and my imagination made an effort to convert the swiftly moving station wagon into a winged palfrey. The whole episode was a witches' brew and I was all for taking a deep draught of it but at every break an overfed, over fat Mexican policeman lurched against me bringing me back to reality. My winged horse was a rubber-tyred reality, and there was no palfrey in the souls of any of my captors.

There was little or no conversation in the beginning but I sensed what I thought to be a measure of unease in the party. A consciousness of violating, officially, the legal sanctions of a national of another country, a national about whose importance or unimportance no one would quite determine.

Shortly before midnight we stopped for gasoline. Also we all went into the store for coffee. I had not been handcuffed. Indeed I am assured that handcuffs are illegal in Mexico. I am given to believe it this time since it aids in the disposal of troublesome prisoners by the operation of what is known as 'Lay Fuga', the law of flight. A shot in the back, a story of attempted flight, and none to dispute it.

Coffee seemed to improve matters for everybody. It set a better tone and conversation grew as the miles passed. No one seemed willing to answer my questions or give any explanation. The presence of the American officers gave me some reassurance whenever I thought of the many stories I had been told of similar disappearances in Mexico. The route was obviously northward; we came ever nearer the civilized United States.

We continued on through the night maintaining a high rate of speed. Occasionally we would stop for gasoline at which times the driver would be relieved and on we went all through the following day. From time to time we became almost jolly—talking and singing and from time to time one or another's dozing where possible and so far as the speed of the car permitted. In many rides in many counties, and despite the circumstances, those 750 miles will stand out as the most beautiful of any I have yet taken.

I learned later what transpired following my departure. I inject it here to make clear what occurred as we approached the US border late the second evening of this virtually non-stop flight.

My secretary had tried to contact me the morning following our departure, and finding me again missing, reported it to the lawyers. They, guessing what had happened, went at once to a judge of an appropriate court and laid the matters before him.

This judge became incensed at what he termed the 'high-handed methods of U.S. officials exercising tutelary activities in Mexican affairs' and set about putting a stop to this specific example of it. He wired an order to all border points instructing the officers to stop the car and take into custody all officers and myself and hold for investigation.

Shortly after dark some twenty-four hours after setting out we arrived at a small customs office standing within Mexico some ten miles south of Laredo. Here we were stopped and the senior of the two U.S. officers and the chief of the Mexican officers went with the Customs house staff. We waited for a long time and I could hear the crank of the telephone bell from time to time. There were occasional powwows held with the driver and then back he would go with the telephone soon. Thinking of what I had suspected to be their unease at the commencement of the trip, I had the impression they were telephoning Mexico City. Perhaps they did, but after nearly two hours' wait a large U.S. customs limousine drove up at a furious pace and a man stepped out quickly and went directly into the Customs House. In a few minutes they all came out and the senior of the two U.S. officers went with the men newly arrived from the north and the others came with the Mexican officer and got back into the station wagon. The limousine turned and shot off to the north again. We also turned and shot off to the south back towards where we had come from and going at a terrific pace. It seemed that we were headed back to Mexico City. Of course I bombarded the offers with questions while it was of no use. I could feel a change in tempers. All were tired and worn from the long unbroken drive of the whole night and day. The answers I received were not merely pointers in information, they became threatening.

After going for perhaps twelve miles back upon the road we had so recently traveled, we suddenly slowed down and turned sharply to the east through an opening in the bush. There was no road here, but a trail quickly led us to the bed of a dry river and into this we eased ourselves and set off following the course of the river bed, which for all the world resembled a ride through a quarry. The lurching of the car now became a torture to me, as first the man on my right and then the man on my left would be almost in my lap and continuously I was tightly squeezed between these over-sized specimens of humanity.

We were now deep in a wilderness of no man's land and I became seriously alarmed. Was I to become a victim of the infamous 'Lay Fuga' I asked myself? Almost I wished for the comparative security of my original cell in Mexico City. The speed had now dropped to no more than a fast walk. All tempers dropped alarmingly, including my own. We had now been scarcely thirty hours continuously traveling, without sleep and without rest. My insistent demands threatened my own destruction but I had become almost reckless. On one occasion the chief of the Mexicans pulled his long pistol from his holster and taking hold of it by the barrel, threatened to smack it across my face if I as much as opened up once more. I subsided, but do what I could, I could make no sense to this expedition into this remote wilderness. We were still in the river bank and had been now for several hours and there seemed to be no end to it. I was distinctly opposed to disappearing without a trace and of course I had no knowledge of the events which had occurred in Mexico City since I had left. To me this was the River Styx and I was already a dead man. We had been going over this route for some five hours or so—by the time it had come to resemble a trip on stormy waters in a small rowboat and where we climbed the bank, we shortly found ourselves on a road leading into what seemed the ghost town. It was perhaps four o'clock in the morning and as yet no signs of daylight. The moon which had only intensified the eeriness of the desolate area through which we traveled was now set and as yet no sign of daylight.

From the excited conversation which arose in the car upon our entering this habited area, it seemed plain that our party had lost their way and were casting about for someone to direct them. The entire place seemed asleep and in darkness. We pulled up at a house whose front door was open; a chair laid on its side blocked the entrance as if to keep out wandering cattle. One of our number got out and knocked on the door jamb with the butt-end of his pistol and immediately there appeared a man fully dressed, just as if he had been awaiting our arrival. He was unable to help us so we moved on, stopping further down the street. Here the same situation occurred. A chair was athwart the open entrance and this time it was a woman who appeared, silently and immediately and also fully dressed. I wondered did all Mexicans here go to bed fully dressed.

The person likewise was unable to direct us and again we moved on. We crept slowly down what became the main thoroughfare of the town. There stepped out of the night and into the glare of our headlights, the local constable or whatever name the law is represented by in such places. Even he, however, was unable to direct us but he went off to get La Capitaine who did know the way. When the Capitaine arrived he started to describe the route when the mission officer who was already out of the car and who was still carrying his pistol in his hand indicated to him to get in.

To me it appeared like an order and so it seemed Le Capitaine so interpreted it, so he stepped meekly in and off we drove once more, this time with assurance of our direction.

I had been somewhat relieved to discover that we had a real destination and not merely some remote spot in the desolation through which we had some where my bones could rot, unknown and unknowing.

In the light of what I learned later it became obvious that news of the Judge's telegraphed order had become known to our party at the small customs office. We had taken across-country to a small point of legal entry into the U.S. which was not served by telegraph and where consequently there would be no one to say them nay.

When we arrived at the small bridge at Zapota, still in the darkness of the early morning, I got a glimmering of what had happened and I was about to conclude that this was the final curtain on my Mexican drama. Then an event occurred which formed a most fitting climax to this over-engineered attempt to get me into the U.S., this bizarre travesty of international cooperation between (very) independent agencies of two adjoining 'good neighbor' countries. Tired as I was, and sorry for me with a petrified self pity, the final act of the drama could only have happened elsewhere with a Gilbert & Sullivan production and I found great refreshment and even greater amusement in its enactment.

I think perhaps my loud, uncontrolled laughter avoided an international incident.

We drove up to the administration officer of the Mexican end of this bridge which crossed the Rio Grande at a narrow point. Our party, stiff and sore from their long ride, pulled up and stepped out of the car. There were of course no lights showing as the bridge was closed for the night—there being only a day-time staff here and for a moment there was some indecision as to the next move.

The next move came from the deep shadows of a nearby building in the shape of seven men armed with an assortment of rifles, revolvers, and Tommy guns. Our party was ordered, in mixed English and Spanish, to hold up their hands. The leader of our party reached for his badge to show his authority. Unfortunately for him the pocket in which he kept his badge was in the vicinity of his pistol holster and our new friends did not like his action. His arm was knocked up with the barrel of a rifle. Automatically he again reached for his badge and again, and with more emphasis, his arm was knocked up.

It was here that I laughed loud and long. My laughter probably had some hysteria in it for I was worn almost to a state of collapse. However the laugh seemed to indicate that something was wrong and the opposing parties started talking.

It transpired after armistice negotiations were under way and the big, circular legend 'Republic of Mexico' painted on the station wagon had been pointed out, that the town constable who had been left behind so abruptly, and who had seen 'La Capitaine' so abruptly put into the car at the point of a revolver as it were, had telephoned ahead of us to warn that a gang of enemy agents of some sort had kidnapped his chief so that the party was then on its way to blow up the Zapata bridge.

Thus it was that my Mexican odyssey came to a colorful conclusion. We crossed the bridge into the U.S. and drove up the American side of the Rio Grande back to Laredo where I was interrogated by an Immigration Board of Enquiry at which Uncle Sam conducted a tawdry burlesque. For months I had been crossing the border with passport in perfect order. In fact I had crossed twice during the previous three weeks going by air from New York to Mexico City and returned duly exhibiting my passport visas and at no time had I been illegally in either the U.S.A. or Mexico.

Notwithstanding this and notwithstanding the fact that I had been brought into the U.S. by force and, as American officers admitted, without being given an opportunity of securing my personal belongings and my passport. The Board of Enquiry concluded their farce with a recommendation to Washington that owing to the fact that I had entered the U.S. at Zapota without a passport I be deported to Canada when the authorities had done with me.

At a later date both Secretary of State Hull and Attorney General Biddle in an interview with my lawyer from New York agreed that the episode was of a nature to reflect upon the operations of a law agency of a great state and that it 'left a bad taste in this mouth.'

But unfortunately they neither of them specified whose mouth.

Thus ends Ernest's account of his Mexican adventure. Legal documents (in the U.S. Archives) state that A.E. Dawson was first arrested in Mexico City on October 15, 1943. The U.S. documents are rather vague about his and Forbes's transport to the United States, stating only that "Thereafter they were brought to [Northern District of] Texas from where they were removed to this district [Southern District of New York] to await trial."

There is no record of any Mexican court appearances on the U.S. request to Mexican authorities for Dawson and Forbes's arrests in Mexico. No record exists of their "extradition" to the U.S. The entire matter seems to have been extremely informal, if not downright illegal.

MUCH WANTED MEN EXPELLED FROM MEXICO

SYDNEY, Australia ⊙— William McKell, premier of New South Wales, said today action is being taken to have John Woolcutt Forbes, wanted on a £461,500 fraud charge, returned to Australia following arrest in Mexico City. He said Forbes disappeared from Australia early in 1939.

The Mexican Government last night announced that three men arrested Saturday in Mexico City on request of the United States Treasury Department were ordered expelled from Mexico, and "probably are already in United States."

Police said the three were wanted by the United States, Canada and Australia on confidence games charges involving more than $2,000,000.

They gave their names as John Woolcutt Forbes, Alfred E. Dawson and Irving Garfunkel. The Mexican government announcement gave their names as George Blake Irving, Alfred Ernest Dawson and Irving Varney, but the police said that Washington had informed them that Forbes might be using the name of George Blake, George De Place or George Smith.

The man wanted by Canada is Dawson. Inspector E. Fell of the Foreign Exchange Board has announced in Toronto that Dawson, a Toronto stock broker, faces a charge of illegally exporting $70,000 in cash.

A.E.Dawson and John Woolcott Forbes' case was covered extensively by newspapers all over Canada, and the United States, from Florida to British Colombia. This story appeared in the Nanaimo Daily News, October 27, 1942. Newspapers all over Australia also covered the story.

SWINDLER GOING HOME

Will Be Tried in Australia for an Alleged $10,000,000 Fraud

John Woolcott Forbes, Australian financier who recently pleaded guilty here to cheating investors in this country, will be sent back to Australia for prosecution there in an alleged $10,000,000 swindle, following action taken yesterday by Federal Judge Alfred C. Coxe. On the motion of Joseph Brandwen, Assistant United States Attorney, who acted at the behest of Secretary of State Cordell Hull and Attorney General Francis Biddle, Judge Coxe reduced Forbes's five-year sentence to the time served.

Forbes was not released but will be held in Federal custody until transportation is arranged for him and an Australian police sergeant who came here to get him.

The New York Times
Published: May 20, 1943

A.E Dawson and John Woolcott Forbes were headline stories in major newpapers such as The New York Times and the Globe and Mail.

CHAPTER 17:
Trials and Punishment

After the surreal excitement of the Mexican adventure, things got very real, very fast. The three men—Ernest, Forbes, and a man named Garfinkle (or Perry)—fell into a humiliating and exacting justice system, with its lengthy prison stays, lawyers' fees, and very real evidence.

The Mexican authorities said that their immigration documents were "not in order" and that the men had been expelled from Mexico at the request of the United States Treasury authorities.[115] The announcement stated, "On examining their documents... they were invited to leave the country."

Right.

In actual fact, Ernest and the others were apparently kidnapped, without a court hearing, and with varying explanations from Mexico and the U.S. In one newspaper account, their papers were not in order and the Mexican government ousted the men. In other accounts, the U.S. made a formal extradition request. In Ernest's account, there was to be a hearing, but the men were summarily pushed into a Mexican government station wagon and shipped north to Texas. And according to Ernest, the Mexican government was divided in its response, given its confused reactions at the border.

I believe Ernest's account. It would be hard to make up such detail, even for a practised writer.

Whatever the background was, the whole business of being shipped back to the U.S. seems to have been extra-judicial, if not downright illegal. And

---

115 *The Ottawa Journal*, "Toronto Broker Said Expelled From Mexico," October 27, 1942.

even though American officials later admitted to having a "bad taste in the mouth" about the affair, they ignored the problems and continued with their prosecution proceedings.

On October 24, 1942, the three men were detained in Mexico City and summarily moved, without a hearing, by Mexican and American authorities to Texas. There, they were formally arrested on U.S. soil on charges of forging and uttering the signature on a United States Treasury cheque. The U.S. arrests were made on the basis of a single forgery charge by Mrs. Mary Jane Frey and Irving Garfinkel, with at least twenty further counts expected from the grand jury in New York City.

While the men were first held in the U.S. on "technical" charges, the consequences were tangible and inescapable.

U.S. Secret Service agent Forrest V. Sorrels arrested Forbes and Dawson, both alleged to be fugitives from New York City at the time. The Secret Service was involved because that agency, since its early days in the late 1800s, had been given the charge of investigating and enforcing financial crimes and fraud in the United States. (Today, the Secret Service is much better known for its role in protecting the president and other high officials. It still, however, acts on financial fraud.) Given the SEC's eagerness to catch a Canadian fraudster, it is not surprising that U.S. Secret Service agents were activated in Mexico City to catch him and transport the men to U.S. soil in Texas for arrest.

An extradition request from Canada stated that Dawson, Forbes, and Perry were also fugitives from justice in Canada. Ernest and Perry were later moved to Canada to face charges, while Forbes was extradited to Australia to face charges there.

What were the men doing in Mexico? One newspaper account[116] said that "Forbes and Dawson were preparing to exploit a piece of mahogany land, a thousand miles from nowhere, when they were apprehended in Mexico."[117] This jives with Ernest's letter to Lynda on the same subject. The forestry deal

---

116 *The Globe and Mail,* "Ontario government today sought to extradite Forbes and Dawson," March 30, 1943.
117 On October 29, 1942, Northern District Texas Judge W. Ravelle signed a warrant for the two prisoners to be removed from the Dallas Jail to the Southern District of New York. U.S. Marshall J.R. Wright moved them.

may have been shady also; the U.S. state attorney stated that the same tract of land had already been the subject of an indictment in Cleveland, Ohio.

On December 4, the grand jury in New York filed twenty-one additional charges of violations of the mail fraud statute, the Securities Act of 1933, of conspiracy, and violations of the Securities Exchange Act of 1934 (not being a registered broker). All of these charges were possible only because Ernest had been on U.S. soil, not in Canada, when the frauds took place.

After the SEC accumulated a long list of mail fraud and registration citations, Lund was able to report[118] success at last in his SEC history: He wrote,

> On December 29, 1942 (Litigation Release No. 48) the SEC announced the indictments of 2 individuals and 3 companies for fraudulently offering securities into the United States from Toronto. The indictment was obtained in the Southern District of New York and charged false representations and failure to register.

Later in 1943, the two defendants pleaded not guilty to the mail fraud charges and conspiracy, and a second indictment of five counts violating the Securities Exchange Act of 1934.

Bail was set at $50,000 for A.E. Dawson and $100,000 for Forbes. Neither posted bail and both were moved to the federal Detention Prison on West Street, in New York City.

The two men eventually changed their pleas to "guilty" and on March 29, 1943, both were sentenced on each of counts 1 through 5, to run concurrently. Ernest received a four-year sentence, Forbes got five. The court records do not say why the difference, but it was probably because Forbes had the direct, personal contact with the victims, and was responsible for the swindle at the individual level. He may have been seen as the instigator of the whole scheme, with Ernest playing a secondary role as the administrator of the frauds.

A newspaper account[119] provided some details of the swindle:

> A Philadelphia man was dying and his wife suffering from a paralytic stroke when Forbes approached them, Brandwen [U.S. States

---

118 Lund, A.H., *The Canadian Problem: Illegal Securities Offerings 1933-1955*, The Securities and Exchange Commission, March 30, 1955, page 39.
119 *The Globe and Mail*, "Dawson and Forbes Sentenced," March 29, 1943.

attorney] told the court, adding Forbes took them for $8000 and left them penniless.

In the end, the New York court heard both Ernest and Forbes plead guilty, during a hearing that took just a few minutes. Ernest probably pleaded guilty because the SEC had irrefutable evidence on the mail fraud counts.

Two lawyers had not succeeded in extricating Ernest from the charges, although the forgery charge was dropped after handwriting analysis. The SEC had the goods on him for the rest of the charges, having envelopes and letters to prove the mail fraud charges. The SEC could probably have produced many irate victims to testify if the matter had gone to trial.

The two men were sentenced to Lewisburg Penitentiary, Pennsylvania, where they served until they were each expedited or deported to their home countries later in 1943.

On November 15, 1943, Ernest's sentence was reduced to time served so that he could be sent back to Canada to face charges from the Ontario Securities Commission in Ontario.[120] There, he pleaded guilty again and was sentenced to four years in the Kingston Penitentiary on March 2 of 1944.[121] No restitution would be made to any of the fraud victims, despite a total fraud of $138,000 in stocks and bonds.

Ernest may have pleaded guilty to avoid the dreadful publicity that would have accompanied a trial, where all the details of his crimes would have been revealed to his—and his family's—community. He was still a gentleman, a man with pride. And perhaps, after having spent half a million dollars in legal fees, Ernest wanted to spare his family the additional shame and expense.

Once in Kingston Penitentiary, Ernest was transferred to Collins Bay Penitentiary. There he settled in for his long sentence.

Medical Condition

At that time, we have only one interesting insight into Ernest's condition. If you look closely at his mug shot from the Kingston Penitentiary (see cover photo), you will notice a swelling of his lower right jaw. Dr. Maninder Sihota, a dentist based in Sherwood Park, Alberta, examined the photographs and

---

120 *The New York Times*, "Term Cut to Face New Charge," November 16, 1943.
121 *The Globe and Mail*, "Dawson Given 4-yr term, Kingston," March 3, 1944, page 21.

diagnosed him as suffering from an abscess of his lower right molar, or the second or third teeth below it.

Dr. Sihota said, "If he were my patient, I would put him on antibiotics, *stat*!"

It is unlikely, however, that Ernest received antibiotics for his dangerous condition. Penicillin was just beginning to be available to civilians a year later. Mass production had been pioneered by the United States for troops during the years of World War II, and Australia first made it commercially available for civilians only in 1945.

Sulfa drugs were widely used for bacterial infections at the time. However, they were not usually used for dental conditions. It is most likely that the tooth would have been extracted and drained.

We don't know how Ernest was treated, if at all, for his abscess. All we know is that he must have suffered great pain at the time, and somehow he survived.

Perry Convicted in Ontario

Like the other two—Dawson and Forbes—Perry apparently fled to Mexico when things got hot in Ontario and the U.S. He was picked up in Mexico City and hustled to the United States in the big Mexican government station wagon. Together the three men were driven north until crossing the Rio Grande, and were formally arrested on U.S. soil in Laredo, Texas.

Perry was held in the United States as a material witness to the crimes of Dawson and Forbes, then deported on February 15, 1943, back to Ontario.[122] There he was tried and convicted on Ontario charges. In Ontario's Simcoe court, before Magistrate H.J. Gillian, Perry pleaded guilty on two charges of fraud and was sentenced to prison. He pleaded not guilty on two other charges. In April 1943 he was found guilty on six of twenty-one Criminal Code counts. The newspaper account stated that the charges were for "obtaining various sums of money, stocks, and bonds by false pretenses," the other six for using documents known to be forged. It is estimated that the 27 charges involved transactions in stocks and bonds between A.E. Dawson

---

122 *Archives of Ontario, file # 1250,* 1942. Letter from W.F. Watkins, District Director, New York District to C.R. Magone, Senior Solicitor, Attorney-General's Department, Toronto, Ontario, Feb. 8, 1943.

& Co and a number of clients totaling $150,000."[123] That would amount to more than two and a half million dollars in today's Canadian dollars.

The judge was not quoted that day in the Perry case, but at the time, the public was certainly angry about stock fraud. The tenor of the times is indicated in a newspaper account that same day, concerning an unrelated case. In that case,[124] the judge pronounced another fraudulent securities salesman as "a slick, smooth salesman," who "definitely went out... to defraud the public and he did the same knowing the whole set-up was a swindle of the public." The same could probably have been said of Perry.

The End of the Forbes Story

Although he was also wanted in Ontario, Forbes was shipped to Australia to face earlier charges there.

Initially Forbes, like Ernest, pleaded not guilty to the U.S. charges, but changed his plea to "guilty" on March 1, 1943. He served a short time in the Lewisburg Penitentiary. On May 19, 1943, Forbes's sentence was reduced to time served so that he could be extradited back to Australia, to be tried on charges of forgery.

Court proceedings against Forbes had continued in Australia, in his absence. He left behind a string of debts and unpaid advances. One account[125] described a typical scene:

> There was laughter in the Bankruptcy Court today when the name "John Woolcott Forbes," was called three times with the resulting statement, "no appearance." The creditor, petitioning against the missing Sydney financier was Producers and General Finance Corporation. Ltd. Justice Lukin declared Forbes bankrupt.

Despite setbacks in court, Forbes was always one step ahead of the authorities. He seemed to have papers and plenty of cash to finance his travels, and was not heard of in the press until two years later, when the U.S. authorities picked him up in Mexico City.

---

123 *The Globe and Mail*, "C.W.C. Perry appears in Simcoe," April 9, 1943.
124 *The Globe and Mail*, "Perry found guilty on six charges under Ontario Securities Act," April 10, 1943, page 24.
125 *Daily Examiner*, "Declared Bankrupt John Woolcott Forbes," April 17, 1940.

Back in Australia, the courts did not entertain for a moment the notion of putting Forbes back on bail.[126] Given his history of jumping bail in Bombay, he was refused bail by the judge who said he was not satisfied that Forbes would not try to escape again, if given the opportunity. "In fact, there is every reason to assume he would break," added the judge.

In Australia, Forbes claimed innocence in the Canadian and U.S. matters.[127] He explained away his part in the fraudulent schemes by blaming Ernest:

> In Canada I engaged in the only business I knew—stocks and bonds. Several months went by when a sense of uneasiness and a haunted feeling drove me into the United States, seeking employment without background.
>
> My wife and children were penniless. My remaining few assets, even my wedding gifts, were swallowed up. In New York I met my late Canadian employer, Dawson. He appeared sound and the stock he gave me to sell appeared sound.
>
> I worked for him with honest faith. But then soon I found his morals had crumbled with bad business practices.
>
> Unwittingly I found I was being used as Dawson's dupe.

This seemingly mendacious account ignores the fact that Forbes was deeply involved in the Canadian indictments with Dawson, whom he had obviously met in Ontario, not New York. The OSC's pending investigation may have prompted the "haunted feeling," perhaps even a hunted feeling! The account also ignores his pleading guilty to many counts in the U.S. It may be true, however, that Ernest's morals had crumbled by that time. And rather than being a dupe, Forbes was clearly a full partner in the operations, if not the lead person, according to both the U.S. and Canadian indictments.

Ernest stated that he had no idea what Forbes was up to. In a letter to Lynda,[128] he wrote as always, the innocent man:

---

126 *The Scona Advocate*, "Bail Refused John Woolcott Forbes," August 10, 1943.
127 *The Globe and Mail*, "Forbes in Australia Claims Used as Employer's Dupe," date unknown, page 19.
128 Dawson, A.E., letter from federal holding prison, New York City, April 1, 1943.

> It seems impossible to get out of my mind the scorn of the grand old judge at some of the things we were jointly charged with and the most of which I of course knew nothing. Yet I was compelled by force of circumstance to plead guilty, in advance. Legally of course I pled guilty, only to the violation of certain sections of certain Acts, not to the commission of specific acts arising therefrom.

When finally put on trial in Australia, Forbes boldly declared his innocence of forging, uttering, and falsifying.[129] He claimed that his problems arose due to "lack of education and poor bookkeeping," and to putting his trust in those who were actually manipulating the system.

Forbes claimed to have bought thousands of Producers and General Finance shares at £35 and they consequently fell to £10. He alleged that an official at the company had confessed forging share certificates. The *Advocate* reported,

> Opening the defence, Mr. Shand, K.C.,[leading counsel for Forbes] said the world had adjudged Forbes guilty of being a heartless financier who had robbed widows, children and orphans… The truth is that he put £110,000 into the P. and G. and that he had more than £100,000 in excess of his debts when he was supposed to have forged these certificates.

Despite these protestations, Forbes was found guilty[130] on charges of forging, uttering and falsifying share certificates of the Producers and General Finance. He was sentenced to five years in jail.

Forbes served time as a model prisoner in Australia, working in the bookbinding shop and later in the dispensary as an assistant. When he was released, newspapers followed him home, eager to watch him after the long drought of Forbes news. Reporters described a day-long celebration (of which the reporters must have been part), saying that he looked "fit and well" and that he had a constant stream of callers, relatives, and friends. Reporters described welcome-home posters drawn by his daughters.

---

129 *The Advocate*, "Woolcott Forbes Denies Guilt," March 15, 1944.
130 *Sydney Morning Herald*, "John Woolcott Forbes Case," May 7, 1947.

It didn't take long, however, for Forbes to be back at his old tricks. By 1952, he was back in bankruptcy court as an undischarged bankrupt.[131] (He was trying to escape his debtors by not paying.) He claimed that while his wife had bought a £22,300 home and a £1000 car, and owned shares, with the help of "several bookmaker friends and relatives," he was unemployed and had no assets. This did not match with his lifestyle, however. Forbes was questioned about his "scale of living and holiday visits to the Surfer's Paradise and Katoomba."

Later in that year, it was disclosed in court[132] that one of Forbes's companies (Consolidated Investment Corporation) had purchased £10,000 in shares and transferred them to his wife. His wife appears to have stood at his side, a useful account-holder for his money, throughout his long, fraudulent career. During the hearings,[133] [134] the judge said, "I am unable to accept the answers and explanations given by Forbes. In my opinion, he is able to answer the questions, but does not propose to do so." Forbes was accused of contempt, and the judge pronounced him "quite willing and ready to lie when it suited him." The court sequestered his unsecured liabilities of £56,383 and assets of £2,580.

Forbes apparently lived a fraudster's life consistently, to the end. An investigator for the attorney general testified before a parliamentary committee the following year. He testified that Forbes was still the "brains behind company rackets" and that Forbes was "still operating."

Forbes fades from newspaper accounts after that.

No account of Forbes's death appears in the newspaper digital archives of Australia. However, he appeared to be in ill health in 1952. At that time, he collapsed with a heart attack, although recovering later.[135]

Whenever he died, John Woolcott Forbes apparently lived unrepentant to the end and was a full participant—and sometimes leader—in Ernest Dawson's stock fraud schemes.

---

131 *Morning Bulletin*, "Woolcott Forbes' Estate," August 6, 1952.
132 *Barrier Daily Truth*, "More Alleged Dealings of John Forbes," December 11, 1952.
133 *Barrier Daily Truth*, "Woolcott Forbes Again," *Feb. 17, 1953.*
134 *The Evening Advocate*, "John Woolcott Forbes Comes Before Justice Clyne," December 15, 1952.
135 *The Argus,* "Forbes Collapses," *September 21, 1952.*

Justice in the End?

In the end, justice was served, more or less, despite Ernest and Forbes blaming each other for the frauds. No doubt, both of them knew what was going on, and both tolerated and depended upon each others' crimes—with Forbes seducing the victims and Ernest doing the paperwork. The justice system ignored their mutual blaming and placed the blame solidly on the two men. Meanwhile Perry was convicted in Ontario too.

In Ontario, Ernest was wanted for stock fraud as well as illegally exporting $70,000 in cash from Canada.

None of the victims, in the U.S. or Canada, received compensation for their losses, despite Ernest's later, brief, regrets in prison. The total losses would have amounted to between five and ten million dollars in today's dollars.

In the end, the three men surrendered their freedom and reputations for their crimes. The price for Ernest was the highest, since he regarded himself as a man of intellect, a man of principle, and a man of good standing.

All that was lost when the doors of the penitentiary clanged shut behind him.

CHAPTER 18:
The Orkis Novel– Ernest Looks Back

In his early seventies, long after his trials and imprisonment, Ernest embarked on one last, great literary journey. He wrote a 355-page, 130,000-word novel. It was a huge work that summed up his beliefs as they stood during the 1920s: his take on Canada, the United States, and the world, and his idealized views on love between men and women.

The book, unpublished, is a coming-of-age story about a young Canadian woman, Janet. At the same time, the book is a Victorian-style Harlequin romance, complete with a flawed hero, George.

The novel is written in rather formal English, compared to modern writing. One can almost hear Ernest as one reads it… the deep, baritone voice of an old man, speaking in a dignified, measured pace. It takes awhile to get used to the prose, but the modern reader can become comfortable with it and read the entire novel. Like the rest of the materials in Ernest's wooden trunk, the novel told nothing of his criminal activities or the dark periods of his life. It tells much, however, about the man's childhood, his ideals, and his views of the world before the Great Depression.

Ernest called the book *In the Shadow of Orkis*.

Orkis is an imaginary village in rural Ontario with one central industry— a boy's prep school. It doesn't take too much imagination to call up the real Grove (or Lakefield) School, where Ernest sent his boys to be educated. This idyllic, imaginary school enjoys an enlightened headmaster, Dr. James

Ault, who adopts the infant Janet when both her parents die in an automobile accident.

The story opens on Janet's twenty-first birthday, when she comes into a substantial inheritance from her long-dead parents. On the same day, she learns of a three-year-old boy whom she is soon to "adopt" when his parents are sent to Singapore by the British Admiralty—an unsuitable place for a child, apparently. The boy's name is Christopher, but he is quickly nicknamed Christopher Robin by everyone in Orkis.

Janet meets George, a troubled World War I veteran visiting Canada, an Englishman. George suffers from what we would now call post-traumatic stress disorder, PTSD, and a painful bayonet wound to his head. He is a businessman who eventually invests in a mine near Orkis.

Janet and George get to know each other slowly and tentatively over three hundred pages. While it becomes clear that the two are meant for each other, they approach their relationship with Victorian caution and high moral purpose. Not until page 353 do they actually kiss.

George is captivated by Canada and settles in Orkis after deciding to invest there and move from London. A crisis ensues when George's medical condition becomes unbearable, and he is taken to New York City for possibly fatal surgery. He does not declare his intentions to Janet, fearing to burden her with his medical condition. When he receives successful treatment for his bayonet wound, he finally explains and asks her to marry him. He also loves the little boy, Christopher, and presumably all three live happily ever after.

Looking for Clues About Ernest

It seemed that reading the novel might illuminate Ernest's character—the manuscript might reveal something about its author in 355 pages. I certainly hoped so because it took a week to read the bulky manuscript.

However, nothing much happens in the first hundred pages. We are introduced to all the wonderful people of Orkis. Every one of the characters—Uncle James and Aunt Bess, the local businessmen, the banker, the storekeeper, and the boys at the school—every person is a *nice* person. There is not a single nasty character among them. I began to understand why the editor at MacMillan told Ernest, in a rejection letter, that the book lacked "tension." (It's hard to build an interesting plot with no villains.) And as for the "lack of reality," also mentioned by the editor, it was clear that Ernest had created an unrealistic world of only nice people, not a world in which people came with various degrees of selfishness, dishonesty, sexism, laziness, greed, stupidity and evil. All Ernest's characters were hard-working, introspective, unselfish, kind, honest, intelligent, and loving. And above all, they embodied "small L" liberal values in their politics.

A determined reader, I read on despite this panoply of virtue.

Like the rest of the wooden trunk, the novel gives no clues as to why Ernest "went bad." Just as his letters and essays ignored his legal troubles, his novel does too. By the time he was an old man writing about Orkis, he had managed to forget that he had cheated widows and stolen from retired farmers. The novel contains no purposeful wrongdoing, no guilt, and no evil. Ernest had simply wiped away that portion of his life from his reality. While "bad things" happened to characters, such as George's combat experience in World War I, the characters overcame their adversities.

George says, "I hope I shall never again experience the long hours of physical discomfort of life in the trenches, yet it was there I found my greatest escape from myself, as one of a hundred men in a trench awaiting the dawn, there was, as you say, a sense of needing someone and of being needed. Of belonging and of being counted on." Ernest's equivalent of this experience might have been his time in prisons. There he faced the abyss that his life had become and may have occupied himself by observing and engaging in the lives of his fellow prisoners.

An Autobiographical Novel

The novel told me about many other things though. Various characters described actual parts of Ernest's life that we already knew about. Like most first-time novelists, he wrote an autobiographical novel. In the novel, the characters described how Ernest might have felt about this early life.

For instance, the character George describes his early life. Janet asks him:

"Have you had a happy childhood, George?"

He looked a little surprised at the question and did not immediately answer. When he spoke, it was with a sort of wistfulness which made Janet think of Christopher Robin. She could not have said why.

"Not in the sense that I think you mean, Janet. I have had good health, which is of course, important, and I have no personal sorrows or griefs of any moment. My mother died too early for me to remember her and my father died also, a few years ago. *He was not particularly interested in his children. My sister and I have never had a real home, that is, as children*...[emphasis added]

"*I frequently get a hunger for some real home life*, especially when I see households like that of Dr. Ault [Uncle James]; environed with the natural things which make for happy living."

This could easily have been Ernest, thinking of his childhood, as described by his sister Daisy in her book. He and his siblings were a sad lot, ignored by parents who were immersed in their enthusiasms for the church and amateur theatre, and then came a hated stepmother. Ernest repeatedly ran away from this unpleasant home.

Later, perhaps, he realized that his wife Lynda was giving his own children a real home life, despite his own high-risk business life and being on the road much of the time. He was extremely grateful to his wife for creating a stable home life he had so badly wanted for himself.

Elsewhere in the novel, George tells of growing up in England and his awakening to Canada, its promise, and its contrast to England. The character George, probably like Ernest, had been intrigued by Canada's public relations campaign to attract settlers. He explains to Janet:

"Years ago, this country [Canada] was the centre of an effort to induce emigration to Canada and huge posters were placarded all about in railway stations and elsewhere, showing large wheat fields and rich pastures. I became fascinated with them and decided I would learn farming, with the idea of going to Canada.

"The decision came about in a curious way. I had stopped to stroke the nose of an old dappled grey horse in the shafts of a low cart, when two girls stepped up into the cart. They were about to drive off when I asked them if they were from a farm. I had the idea they were because there were two milk cans in the cart. They were from their father's farm, a few miles out. They delivered milk in town and were now going home.

"I enquired if they thought I could work there. They thought their father wanted a boy and suggested I ride out with them. I jumped in at once and quickly got the job. There and then I envisioned myself as a farmer of wide, limitless expanses of land, much as I had seen in the huge posters. However, I went into business instead, later..."

"How old were you then, George," he was asked.

"Not quite thirteen," he answered.

In fact, according to Ernest's sister Daisy, he and his sisters had determined at a young age to emigrate to Canada. Like George, they must have seen those big posters. And, in fact, as a teen, Ernest left London and went out to Derbyshire to learn farming—probably to prepare for a rural life in Canada. In the novel, George describes his early farming experience as they travel through Derbyshire. And in fact, Ernest's first job in Canada was on an Ontario farm.

In the novel, Ernest describes the mindset of a London child and the difficulties of clearing land for farming in forested, rocky Ontario.

It is quite impossible for a person born and brought up anywhere on the American continent to realize the extent of, the total and complete ignorance of the average London child concerning matters rural. Even in the largest American cities, New York, Chicago, Philadelphia, a child hears about farms and forests; has relatives or friends who are familiar with country life by some form or another of actual experience. The pioneer tradition still is known and recognized on Broadway, State Street or Penn Avenue. But to the average London child, for all he knows or comprehends, the whole world consists of paved streets, tramcars and tall policemen. Water comes from taps:—that is his right. Milk is brought to the back door, if there is a back door. Meat hangs on hooks in butcher shops; and, to get bread, one has to take off a paper wrapper. As in some far away dream he has heard of cows, sheep, pigs, hay and growing grain, but it was a very far away dream, having no existence in fact.

Christopher Robin found himself in what was, to him, a strange and fascinating world. It was a far cry from Hyde Park Crescent where he had to hold someone's hand always when he went outdoors. A far cry from there to this village of Orkis at the edge of an almost primitive backwoods country...

Throughout the wide region to the north were settlers and farmers, but there was relatively little land capable of cultivation except by the most strenuous efforts. The land had first to be cleared of trees and stumps, large heavy stones removed, new crops of which would be plowed up each year. Much of what little grain was grown had to be out with a cradle, and the hay with a scythe:—a heavy way of life, especially for men who could not resist the lure of the hunt for more than a few days at a time.

Until one reads the novel, it is hard to realize how much his years of rural life had stayed with Ernest. In his old age, his mind went back to his rural rather than his city roots. Even his early days in insurance took him to rural Ontario. To him, there was something pure and good about living in the countryside. That is perhaps why he fought so hard—even to becoming a criminal—to support his boys' idyllic education in rural Lakefield prep school.

Throughout the book, Ernest reinforces a positive view of Canada. George, an Englishman like Ernest, says:

> That is the burden of my complaint against England, my own country. England is stodgy, reluctant to change; it prefers that bad conditions shall continue, rather than they should try something new. It's stupid. I'd fire a man more quickly for doing nothing in a difficult situation, than for making a mistake trying to do something to meet it... I remember asking for an opinion from a group of people over there about a proposed change of routine

that offered hopes of improvement. I got an answer from the Chairman, something along this line:

"Speaking for myself, I think I might venture to say that I am disposed to an affirmative attitude, with reservations." Over here, we would say: "Hell, let's try it."

This brief passage tells us about Ernest, the risk-taking man of action. Another passage tells much about the kind of businessman he was. Janet's "Uncle" Hector says:

"I have spent forty years mixing among the top strata of business men and I have found that among these top men there are two distinct and separate kinds. Practically all the important business men I know belong to one or the other of two categories. One category embraces the creators, and the other the administrators.

"Some men, strong in character and powerful in energy, both mental and physical, are destined to spend their efforts in building,—and leaving when built—businesses for other men to administer and carry on, soundly and surely; men whose character is more suitable for the less exciting but almost as exacting job of administration.

"You will find everywhere large business enterprises of national importance administered capably and well by men who could not possibly have originated those businesses. Such men are temperamentally unfit for the risks and uncertainties of new beginnings."

There is no doubt that Ernest himself was one of the "creator" kind of businessman. He got into trouble trying to be a mere administrator in insurance, and the administrator of his stock market schemes. He was good at starting businesses, but not so good at maintaining them.

A Fundamental Loneliness

We don't know how Ernest came to know the mental state of George, the war-torn veteran. He describes PTSD rather accurately in George. Prison might have had a parallel effect on Ernest, an older, refined gentleman suddenly finding himself for more than four years in the general population of Collins Bay Penitentiary. In the novel, George recalls:

> "Suddenly I found myself a minute figure in a great army, training for something I had never contemplated—a life I loathed with every fibre of my being.
>
> "Except for a few months in hospital as a result of Jerry sticking his bayonet in my head, just behind my ear," he reflexively fingered his wound, "I had four years of hell. Four years of association with fellows, good chaps they were, but fellows who got on my nerves as much as the exploding shells.
>
> "When it was over, I was a mass of suppressed emotions, distorted view points, restless, uneasy, and, perhaps, a little bitter. I wanted badly to come to some such place as this,—I still do—where I could get away from my fellow man. I had no home to return to, no intimate friends to whom I could lay bare what bothered me. My sister had married a man who became a soldier like myself, and I could not project myself into their privacy. I went back to work…
>
> "I have come to dislike crowds and crowded places intensely. I am not a congenial member of a city community, not at all a-man-about-town. Among the scores of men and women I know in London, there is not one to whom I could bring myself to unburden a fraction of what I have unloaded upon you this evening."

Certainly, after his parole, Ernest would have found few, if any, contemporaries to whom he could talk about prison life. His post-prison life must have been as lonely as his prison life.

Ernest's Views of the World

In many ways, Ernest's novel is not merely a romance. He spends many pages considering international relationships among Canada, Great Britain, and the United States. Looking at the future, George and others predict Canada's predicament as an American neighbour. Early in the book, businessman Dewar observes:

> "I know America and Americans very well. I think the informed American citizen part of the salt of the earth, but I'm afraid I share your doubts in this connection. The people of the U.S. make politics their chief pastime; local politics their major preoccupation.
>
> "Anything that they consider outside their concern they are apt to ignore. If it does not appear to concern them, then, for them, it does not exist. They have acquired front rank in power and in importance, but have not yet had time to learn the lessons of international responsibility."

Later, Janet brings up the matter again with George. She asks how it could be bad to live near a country with no territorial ambitions, and yet powerful. George replies:

> "There is such a thing as economic aggression. The United States has no need of more territory; but, suppose that country were to substitute economic imperialism for political imperialism, it could be even worse than military or political domination. They would have the power without the responsibility.
>
> "The United States has enormous resources, unbounded energy and limitless courage. It is a dynamic people. It has everything, everything except a necessary breadth of experience in world affairs. In their phenomenal rapidity of growth, they have not learned, as a nation, that they can only really prosper as the world conditions may permit."

Janet asks if Canada's relationship with Britain might diminish due to U.S. economic interests. George replies:

> "… the danger does not arise from the probability of deliberate intent so much as from inexperience. Power in the hands of even a good man can be dangerous if he lacks experience.

"The United States is in need of a few generations of experience in world affairs and world responsibility. Their very importance, their very power, may thrust that responsibility on their doorstep one day. If it should not come too soon, they may rise and meet it.

"It is the one country in the world where anything can happen. They could: they may yet, astonish the world with their capacity for comprehension. For the present, however, they hold the idea that they can continue to live unto themselves, exporting their surplus goods, taking only money in payment."

George's assessment—no doubt Ernest's own—of the United States and Canada's relationship could easily have been written in 2021

The Novel, an Exercise

Ernest must have devoted hundreds of hours to composing, typing, and revising this manuscript. He submitted it only to MacMillan, and let it rest after their rejection. He deposited the manuscript in the wooden trunk, for his heirs to explore fifty years later.

Epilogue

One can only imagine the awkwardness of Ernest's homecoming after all those years in prison. Perhaps he took the bus from Kingston to Glen Williams. Possibly his son Allen drove to Collins Bay to pick him up. Either way, it was a journey into a new universe for Ernest.

The first days must have been very difficult. He would have arrived at Glen Williams, a home he had never stepped foot in before. His wife had sold the Toronto house and moved to the country. Ernest arrived with a suitcase full of papers he had written and little else. He would have been wearing the same worn suit, tie, and fedora hat that he had worn when he was arrested years before. He had probably lost weight in prison, and the suit hung loosely on his frame.

Glen Williams was a small, rural acreage, far from Toronto, with a huge garden in front and to the side of the house. This was Lynda's new kingdom. In the back, behind the barn, the blue Credit River flowed peacefully, curving its way through a quiet river valley. It was a country idyll, a place of privacy and solace from the shame and the pressures of Toronto. It must also have been a startling sanctuary from prison life.

The change must have been hard for Lynda, too. After nearly a decade of managing home and family on her own, and sleeping alone, suddenly her husband had reappeared. How did they negotiate their new roles with each other? What was his place in this rural world, where so much of life revolved around the garden, the daily meals, and housekeeping? How would the church community in Georgetown receive him, a community where Lynda played a prominent role as organist and choir leader? It was a simple life, but one in which Lynda was in charge.

It took a few years. In the end, Ernest gravitated back to Toronto, where he lived in an apartment of his own and commuted back to Glen Williams on the weekends. He got to know the crew of grandchildren who visited the country home. For a couple of years, he toyed with the idea of starting a Canadian publishing business. Finally, however, he was taken in by a man known to the family only as "Mr. Ruben." Ruben was a stockbroker and he hired Ernest in some ancillary capacity.

Upon his conviction, there is no doubt that Ernest would have lost his licence as a securities salesman. From letters to his sister Madge, however, it seems he could talk up securities sales, although he could not actually close the deals. Mr. Ruben had to sign off on actual sales. On his death certificate, Ernest was listed as a "business consultant."

A Salesman to the End

My last memory of my grandfather Ernest was one of his rare trips west, when he presented his son Don, my father, with a one-pound box of bat guano. Bat guano is the nutrient-rich bat excrement occurring in huge deposits, by the thousands of tons, near ancient bat caves around the world. In times before synthetic fertilizer, guano was extremely valuable. The guano Ernest was peddling—the stock, actually—was packaged in colourful boxes as a houseplant fertilizer. For a while in the late fifties, this bat guano company, United States Guano Corporation, was the latest rage in mining stocks. The Arizona operation began in 1957 and in a bat cave in the Grand Canyon, where mining engineers estimated 100,000 tons of the nitrogen-rich fertilizer had accumulated over the centuries. The mine relied upon an expensive, elaborate tramway built across the canyon to transport mine workers to the site and to transport guano for shipping to Kingman, Arizona. There it was packaged.

The container notes, on Ernest's bat guano box, said, "United States Brand Bat Guano is taken from deposits estimated to be 75,000 to 500,000 years old! Composted in ancient caves at spectacular Granite Gorge of the Grand Canyon, Bat Guano is removed and transported over two miles across the Canyon via the world's longest single span cable tramway."

My father did not buy the bat guano securities Ernest was hawking. It was just as well. Ernest's sister Madge may have bought some of the stock, however. In a letter to Ernest she wrote, "I planned to buy a few shares for my grandchildren to tuck away..." She added that "I said you did not sell stock. I mentioned that a Mr. Ruben was the man I had heard of as the motivating spirit out here. Mr. Smith said the stock as of yesterday morning was 'one and five-eighths'... I told him to call me again about the middle of August when I might be ready to purchase a little of the stock. I was casual, but cagey."

The minable guano deposit turned out to be only 1,000 tons, and the operation shut down in 1960. It never turned a profit. Today the mine is a quaint industrial tourist site in the Grand Canyon National Park.

Bat guano, sadly, was just another one of Ernest's "hot" mining operations that came to naught.

Eventually, the strain of Ernest's business life took its toll on his marriage and family life. As he grew old, he separated from Lynda and remained alone in a small apartment or room in Toronto. According to his grandson Don Dawson (son of Ken Dawson), it was really just a room, and he gradually grew ill with dementia. Don, then twelve years old, remembers his grandfather well because the old man used to come every week to visit his son Ken and play gin rummy. Don says he was still bright, intelligent, and loved to hold conversations on the issues of the day. Don said that on every visit, he would pull out a worn picture of Lynda from his wallet and show it around. "My wife," he would say, with pride.

As his dementia worsened, Ernest was moved to the Branson Hospital in Toronto. One family legend says that when they came to get him, it took seven men to hold him down! Young Don remembers visiting his grandfather in the hospital with horror. "It may have been a mental hospital," he says. "I remember cages with mad people in them." Branson Hospital is now part of the North York General Hospital and offers a full range of mental health care.

Ernest died in that hospital on November 29, 1968. He was eighty-one years old and was buried in the Georgetown graveyard where his wife had been buried two years before him.

Don's Response to Ernest's Life

My father, Donald Dawson, was Ernest's youngest son. He loved his father dearly. Nonetheless, when he became a land surveyor, he moved as far west as he could go after World War II. In a way, it was like the way Ernest escaped England and moved as far west as his money would take him.

Don lived and worked in the outdoors as a land surveyor. And he preached honesty to us as children, by word and by example. Perhaps it was a reaction to his father's corruption in Bay Street. But now his children understand why he became a land surveyor, with his solitary life in the bush, far away from the corruption of big cities. His children understand now why he fled the east to start over with a clean name. And we understand his incorruptible honesty, a stark contrast to his father's ethics.

And we understand the story of the boot lace now. Why, as a provincial land surveyor for the government, Don Dawson bought a pair of leather boot laces to secure the end of his metal survey chain. Since he had used only one lace, he submitted an expense claim to the government for just one boot lace, not the pair. This caused great consternation among the government bookkeepers, resulting in an extensive correspondence on the subject. From this story, Don's children learned that their father, unlike their Grandad, was honest to his core.

Thus, in an odd way, by the phenomenon of opposite reactions, Ernest passed on the best to the family. Despite his shady business practices and the shame of his imprisonment, he passed on a certain virtue. He died a broken old man, but one who had paid for his sins. But he had lived a full life, with generous measures of love, despair, art, and adventure.

Investing Today

Today's world in securities has many parallels to Ernest's day. It's still a game, it's still a gamble, and it's still fixated on gold. The Toronto Stock Exchange index changes with the price of gold. Many of the TSX top sellers are in mining and gold, as in Ernest's day.

Instead of printing sales brochures and misleading pamphlets about stocks, today's securities salesmen do it on the internet. A recent study[136] of 100 publicly traded companies found that many advertised "misleading and untrue" financial statements online. Indeed, 77 percent had no policies guiding their disclosure practices online, according to the study. Many companies publish untrue or outright false statements through social media

---

136 *Edmonton Journal*, Craig, Sean, "'Untrue' disclosures hurting investors, CSA says," March 10, 2017, page B1.

websites. Some statements, said the article in a restrained tone, "could have misled investors."

Another recent article described proposed Ontario legislation to guard against "financial professionals who abuse the trust of clients."[137] An advocacy group for retirees said that "wrongdoing is particularly harmful to older investors who cannot make up the losses they suffer from negligent or fraudulent financial advisers."

From the sounds of it, Ernest would probably say, "The more things change the more they stay the same." And he would have been quite at home with a laptop instead of a briefcase.

At the end of all this, I'm content to have discovered what the family secret was all about. My grandfather had, indeed, been a crook. He had defrauded many innocent investors, ignoring the hardships his scheme resulted in, in an arrogant dodge that attracted the ire of authorities on both sides of the border. He was, indeed, a crook. And he went to jail for it all.

He was also my Grandad. The man who introduced me to poetry, who read widely and was probably the first published author in the family. He was an artist of sorts, whose imagination paved the way for my own career as a reporter and writer.

And so, I am grateful to Ernest Dawson. His wooden trunk bequeathed to me a great tale to tell, the story of how one man successful pioneered the Canadian insurance industry and then engineered a heartless, fraudulent system, for a while. A man who brought both great pride and great shame to my family.

It has turned out to be a Canadian adventure worth telling.

---

137 *The Globe and Mail*, Shufelt, Tim, and McFarland, Janet, "Ontario targets unethical financial advisers," April 1, 2018, page B5.

A.E. Dawson (left) never worked as a stockbroker after his conviction. However, he did find employment as an associate with Mr. Rubens, shown here at Dawson's right.

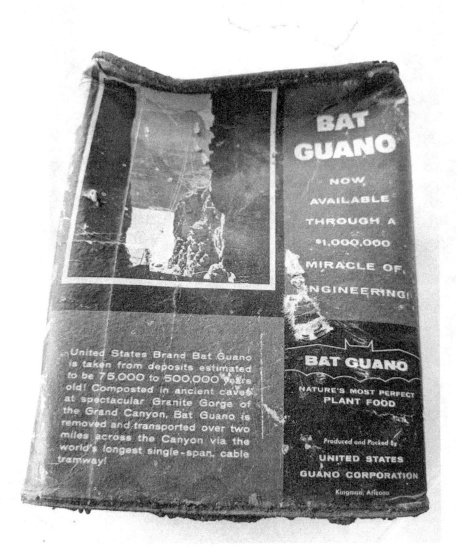

One of A.E. Dawson's last stock gambles was with the United States Guano Corporation. Shown here is a box of bat guano from the Grand Canyon. The product rose briefly in the market but fell even more swiftly. Dawson brought this box to his son, Don, in an apparent sales effort. Don resisted the investment.

*Lynda Knight Dawson was the love of A.E. Dawson's life.
He kept a photo of her in his wallet until his death in 1968.*

Glossary

Advertising Club of New York: Established in 1896 as the Sphinx Club, a group of businesspeople meeting to discuss the advertising industry, establish industry standards, and train advertising professionals. The club established the Better Business Bureau and was home to prominent U.S. businesspeople and politicians. In New York, A.E. Dawson targeted older women and members connected to the club.

Bay Street: The term used for the financial district of downtown Toronto, including banking, stock brokerage, insurance, and other financial activities. A.E. Dawson was a Bay Street stockbroker.

Capital: Funds used to establish and run a company. Capital is raised from investors—shareholders—who share in the capital needs of the company, and eventually in its profits and losses.

Casualty Insurance: A contract between an insurance company and an individual, business, or employer, where the insured pays premiums against the eventuality that the company will pay out funds upon: loss of property; fire, flood, or other damage; and other losses. Casualty insurance includes automobile, liability, agricultural, and theft insurance. In the early 1920s, A.E. Dawson helped establish a major casualty insurance company in Canada and became a prominent spokesperson for the industry. His company pioneered Canadian automobile insurance.

Dividend: A regular payment, typically quarterly, paid by a company to its shareholders from its profits, the amount according to the number of shares

Glossary

owned by the shareholder. In stock fraud, phony "dividends" may be paid to investors from shell companies, or from funds received from other investors.

Exploration: The geological search and evaluation for mineral deposits such as gold, silver, and oil. Exploration requires capital to pay for it, and this is raised through the selling of stocks in legitimate mining companies. Investors essentially bet on hopes that the exploration will yield recoverable mineral deposits.

Great Depression: The decade of the 1930s, when great financial hardship plagued the United States, Canada, and the world. The Great Depression was triggered by the stock market crash of 1929, but was also caused by a weak economic status of the U.S., especially in the automobile and construction industries. People were plunged into poverty, causing severe drops in consumption, and economic activity. A severe drought in the West brought down agricultural production and income. Many banks failed, along with countless other businesses and family farms. The Depression continued until World War II re-stimulated the economy.

Life Insurance: A contract between and individual and an insurance company, where the individual pays regular premiums in exchange for the company's promise to pay a sum of money to the estate upon the death of the individual. A.E. Dawson began his career as a successful life insurance salesman.

Margin: The amount of money borrowed from a broker or a bank to finance the purchase of company stocks. During the 1920s, many people invested "on margin," thanks to low interest rates, a bull market, a culture encouraging speculative investments, and no regulation on the practice. Stocks were bought with a mere 10 to 20 percent down payment on their value. Margin buying increased investors' ability to buy stocks and profit from them, as long as the stock increased in value. However, it also increased the risk of great losses when the stock lost value and brokers or banks made "margin calls," demanding repayment of loans. Many people were ruined when brokers and banks made margin calls after the market crash of 1929. Today, few individuals buy on margin, which is practised mostly by professional investors and large investment firms.

Glossary

OSC: The Ontario Securities Commission. As there was very little federal regulation of Canadian stocks, it was this provincial regulatory body that eventually brought charges of stock fraud against A.E. Dawson & Company.

Ponzi Scheme: A stock fraud where victims are told that they have invested in a stock that is growing in value. They believe this because they receive higher than average returns or "dividends." What is really happening is that the so-called stock is a non-existent enterprise—a shell company—and the "dividend" they receive is money contributed by later investors—who will, in turn, be given money from still later investors. This works for the operator until the pool of investors dries up and there is not enough money to pay off recent investors. The scheme can also collapse if suspicious investors suddenly demand to be paid back. A.E. Dawson appears to have lured investors with phony dividends from shell companies, a Ponzi scheme.

SEC: The U.S. Securities and Exchange Commission. This federal regulatory body brought charges of mail fraud against A.E. Dawson, through a technicality involving using the U.S. Mail Service for the purpose of fraud. In the 1940s, the SEC made great efforts to indict Canadian stock fraudsters who were part of *The Canadian Problem*. A.E. Dawson was one of them.

Secret Service: The United States Secret Service, established in 1865, was originated to fight financial fraud, in particular counterfeiting of U.S. currency. This mission was broadened to protecting the financial and critical infrastructure of the United States, and later to ensure the safety of the president, significant political leaders, and visiting foreign heads of state. It was in its financial mission that the Secret Service apprehended and arrested A.E. Dawson, John Woolcott Forbes, and Perry in Mexico.

Share: A unit of commonly held capital, the basic unit of ownership of a company. The total of all the face values of the company's shares represents the total capital value of the company. The value of a share may or may not represent its market value. A.E. Dawson told investors that the share value of his shell companies was substantial—a good investment—when in actual fact the shares were worthless.

Glossary

Shareholder: A person or institution that owns one or more shares in a public or private corporation.

Shell Company: A company that exists on paper only, but does not participate in any real economic activity, having no significant assets or operations. Shell companies are often used for tax evasion, tax avoidance, money laundering, or to deceive potential investors. A.E. Dawson used a number of shell companies to persuade investors to part with their cash and legitimate company shares.

Stock: Shares of a company made when an investor puts up cash to contribute to the capital needed to run a company. Share values fluctuate according to the perceived value of the company, and shareholders also share in the company's profits and losses. A.E. Dawson "sold" shares of shell companies, as well as legitimate mining operations.

Stockbroker: An individual who buys and sells shares of companies, on behalf of individual investors who entrust the broker with their funds. A.E. Dawson became a stockbroker in 1934 in Toronto's Bay Street, after being forced out of the insurance industry.

Stock Market: A central organization for selling and buying stocks and bonds. In North America, during the 1930s and '40s, the principal market was the New York Stock Exchange. In Canada, the Toronto Stock Exchange and the Montreal Stock Exchange were the principal markets for the selling of Canadian mining stocks.

Stock Market Crash of 1929: The sudden and precipitous loss of value of U.S. and Canadian stocks in October of 1929. Millions of nervous investors abruptly tried to sell their overpriced stocks (most purchased on margin) on October 28, when there were few buyers. As a result, sales of stocks plunged to 40 percent of their overall value in a few days. Continued bad news precipitated continued panic selling. Brokers and banks made margin calls, thus accelerating the rush to sell stocks. While only 10 percent of the American public owned stocks, at the time, the ripple effects of the crash ruined huge numbers of people, worldwide. The crash was followed by the Great Depression, which lasted ten years.

Glossary

The Canadian Problem: The term used by American authorities, in the mid-twentieth century, to describe the widespread practices of Canadian stock swindlers who defrauded American investors. This activity often involved selling "stocks" of shell mining companies. Most of this fraudulent activity was conducted by mail or by long-distance telephone, making it hard for the U.S. to prosecute over the border. A.E. Dawson & Company conducted fraudulent activity in New York City, making it easier for U.S. authorities to prosecute them. Dawson's operations were a classic case of *The Canadian Problem.*

CPSIA information can be obtained
at www.ICGtesting.com
Printed in the USA
BVHW030506280222
630157BV00001B/2